D1525058

Renner Learning Resource Center
Elgin Community College
Elgin, IL 60123

On Love

Also by Rusmir Mahmutćehajić

Krhkost. Sarajevo: Veselin Masleša, 1977.

Krv i tinta. Sarajevo: Veselin Masleša, 1983.

Zemlja i more. Sarajevo: Svjetlost, 1986.

Živa Bosna: politički eseji i intervjui. 1st ed. Ljubljana: Oslobođenje International, 1994.

Živa Bosna: politički eseji i intervjui. 2 ed. Ljubljana: Oslobođenje International, 1995.

Living Bosnia: Political essays and interviews. Trans. Spomenka Beus and Francis R. Jones. Ljubljana: Oslobođenje International, 1996.

O nauku znaka. Sarajevo: DID, 1996.

Dobra Bosna. Zagreb: Durieux, 1997.

Četrdeset kaligrafskih listova Ćazima Hadžimejlića. Sarajevo: DID, 1997.

Kriva politika: Čitanje historije i povjerenje u Bosni. Tuzla: Radio Kameleon, 1998.

Sarajevski eseji: politika, ideologija, tradicija. Zagreb: Durieux, 2000.

Prozori: Riječi i slike. Sarajevo: DID, 2000.

The Denial of Bosnia. Trans. Francis R. Jones and Marina Bowder. University Park: Penn State University Press, 2000.

Bosnia the Good: Tolerance and Tradition. Trans. Marina Bowder. Budapest: Central European University Press, 2000.

Words like wells of colour: Traditional wisdom reflected by the sonnets of Skender Kulenović. Trans. Francis R. Jones et al. Sarajevo: DID, 2002

Sarajevo Essays: Politics, Ideology, and Tradition. Trans. Saba Risaluddin et al. Albany: State University of New York Press, 2003.

Benim Güzel Bosnam. Trans. Zeynep Ozbek. Istanbul: Gelenek Yayinlari, 2004.

Learning From Bosnia: Approaching Tradition. Trans. Saba Risaluddin and Francis R. Jones. New York: Fordham University Press, 2005.

Une réponse bosniaque: Modernité et tradition. Trans. Paul Ballanfat. Zagreb: Durieux; Frankfurt: Textor; Paris: Paris Mediteranee, 2005.

Une Politique Erronée. Trans. Paul Ballanfat. Zagreb: Durieux i Frankfurt: Textor, 2005.

Malo znanja: O drugome u muslimanskim vidicima. Zagreb: Antibarbarus, 2005.

The Mosque. Trans. Saba Risaluddin and Francis R. Jones. New York: Fordham University Press, 2006.

On Love
In the Muslim Tradition

RUSMIR MAHMUTĆEHAJIĆ

Translated by Celia Hawkesworth

Foreword by David B. Burrell, C.S.C.

FORDHAM UNIVERSITY PRESS
NEW YORK 2007

The Abrahamic Dialogues Series, No. 7
ISSN 1548-4130

Library of Congress Cataloging-in-Publication Data

Mahmutcehajic, Rusmir, 1948–
  [O ljubavi. English]
  On love : in the Muslim tradition / Rusmir Mahmutcehajic ;
translated by Celia Hawkesworth.—1st ed.
      p. cm.—(The Abrahamic dialogues series, ISSN 1548-4130;
no. 7)
  Includes bibliographical references.
  ISBN-13: 978-0-8232-2751-8 (cloth : alk. paper)
  ISBN-10: 0-8232-2751-0 (cloth : alk. paper)
  1. Love—Religious aspects—Islam.   2. Islamic ethics.
3. Muslims—Conduct of life.   I. Hawkesworth, Celia, 1942–
II. Title.
BP188.16.L68M3413   2007
297.5′677—dc22

                                        2007006523

Printed in the United States of America
09 08 07 5 4 3 2 1
First edition

In the name of God, the Compassionate, the Merciful

Contents

For her who has a face
of enduring beauty

Foreword

David B. Burrell, C.S.C.

The author of this inspiring reflection, president of the International
Forum "Bosnia"and former vice president of the government of Bosnia and Herzogovina, is an intellectual whose entire life has been en-
gaged in matters of life and death and so has been impelled to reflect
on what makes our lives *human*. In doing so he displays a keen philo-
sophical wit, with a sensitivity honed by his people's suffering as well
as his own. Moreover, he realizes that reflections on something so poi-
gnantly human must reflect a perspective larger than the human to illuminate it. Issues that could be classified as "psychological" in a
western mindset become metaphysical in an Islamic context. So, for
example, with *trust*, a key ingredient to any loving relationship. Taking as his point of departure a passage from the Qur'an, Mahmutćehajić writes:

> We offered Our trust to the heavens, to the earth,
> and to the mountains, but they refused the burden
> and were afraid to receive it. Man undertook to bear it,
> but he has proved a sinner and a fool (Qur'an 33:72).

Refusal of the offered trust is the only reasonable response of
the created to the Creator, if it is based on calculation. That

means accepting being only the recipient of the Almighty, being only His slave. But such a response denies the love whose reasons lie in neither weakness nor power. Neither weakness nor threat can be an obstacle to love. Both the endurance of violence and enterprise, despite their evident madness, remain unknown and despised in relation to the beauty of the Face in which the lover sees himself. No arguments of the reason can participate in that surpassing of duality through the testimony that there is no face other than the Face nor beauty other than Beauty (28).

So God-centered a perspective on *love* can be second nature to Muslims, who are accustomed to praising God for whatever occurs in their lives—events form our perspective, bad as well as good. For the conviction prevails that, however the world unfolds, it is embraced by God's providential care. Yet this is hardly Panglossian or in any way dismissive of the power of humanity to betray that trust. In fact,

human freedom, which makes him a being to whom God as Fullness offers trust, enables him at every moment to revoke every choice of direction. Without the possibility of turning from the Purpose to nothingness, a person is not in trust with God. All that a person has is nothing other than a gift he has received out of Fullness. But, as nothing can be fullness other than fullness itself, a person is essentially a poor man who through his essential emptiness bears witness to his own condition as debtor, for his possibility of stating "there is no fullness other than Fullness" is at the same time his initial orientation towards the resolution of duality in his self (29).

The upshot of this view of the world is that the truth of central human realities like love must be revealed to us, for their place in the universe remains unknown to our powers of reasoning, although that reason can be used to elaborate what revelation—in this case, the Holy Qur'an—leads us to realize about it. Yet our fidelity (or not) to that path lies with us, and the realizations attendant on a faithful following will reveal harmonics in the original revelation unsuspected by ordinary hearers. Mahmutćehajić's fidelity is displayed in these reflections, composed in a style that may often tax our credulity—unless we realize that they are meant to lead us, as well, into an interior appreciation of a love that "moves the sun and moon, and all the stars."

On Love

Paths

A phenomenon is always in a place and time. But it has come from somewhere and goes from there to somewhere. Man as the central phenomenon of existence as a whole can know something of where he has come from and where he is going. In that knowledge there is little certainty, although that is his most significant desire. And that is why the answers to the questions "From where?" "To where?" and "When?" are crucial for the individual, the community, and humanity. They are at the heart of every tradition. Answers to them always also show the way from one pole of existence to another. If these extremes are presented as fullness, which is always one and the same, man is shown to be in a state of returning, where everything along his way is contingent and inconstant.

There can be infinitely many paths toward that fullness, because it is infinitely close to all contingency. It permeates every phenomenon as that phenomenon's primary content. But, man can only know all this from existence in the world, and that means from multiplicity and contingency. He is here a man of the earth and on it. And all human paths on the earth can be right, regardless of whether they cross valleys, mountains, or oceans. All are possible, those that are on the surface, and those that go down into the depths. But each individual reaches a tangible border that he or she cannot pass. Only one path is impossible to travel by physical means. That is the upright path, straight to the sky. That path corresponds to human inwardness. And it seems that it alone determines man as openness.

The questions "Which is the right way?" and "What is the right time?" can have many answers. Two may be singled out as essential. The first is "To survive here and now!" The other is "To be happy here and now!" Both answers are incomplete. First, because every death is in some "here and now." And no one escapes death. Second, because no happiness is permanent. It is always the permanence of impermanence. As long as a man seeks happiness, it escapes him. And its receding stimulates and reinforces longing, pain, and suffering. At the same time, every "here and now" leads to the limit of the Limitless, where answers from the world have no validity, as the poet says:

> I want to be blind, to see what's behind what I see,
> To be deaf, to catch that undertone of peace,
> To be fingerless, to feel untouch touch me.
>
> And once I've passed beyond that wall-less wall
> Where even my burden of selfhood feels like release,
> Time, only time is flowing, and time is all.
>
> (Skender Kulenović,
> "Beyond the wall-less wall")

And it seems that nothing bears witness to this human orientation toward "the wall-less wall" so much as love. It is the experience of every being. Although it is present in the world of forms, not one of them encompasses it. Although it is the experience of every being, not one can represent it in an image that would include the ways in which it is revealed to others. It is itself, therefore, fullness. It is present in every detail, but not one of them exhausts it. Everything in existence reveals itself with it, and through it everything returns to it as fullness. Wherever it seems clearest, its endurance is briefest. It is therefore in the infinity of the instant and of all time, in the greatest height and deepest depth of corporality.

Love is in the spirit and with it. Whenever love reveals itself, it is the descent of the spirit. But the spirit is hidden, even from the Lord's commandment. Although it is possible in everything and toward everything, love is always oriented away from the fullness of the human self and toward it.[1] That is why unity is its only aim, but its existence is always also separateness. What love reveals is the longing for unity but existence in separation. Love is the path toward unity, the path along which everything speaks of that unity that flows in all things.

Love is what stimulates fullness to reveal itself in divergence. Not thereby betraying oneness, it reveals the hidden in creation and division. In that way, existence, with all its details and changes, is the manifestation of fullness as a consequence of existence's love for fullness.

But, love cannot be replaced by knowledge. Love is within knowledge and constantly transforms it into a connection with oneness and return to it. As the moon's year enters into the sun's and emerges from it, as everything in existence comes and goes, so too love enters into knowledge and emerges from it, thereby creating constant ebbs and flows of belief in the human self, from hopelessness to existence in the full sense. And nothing in that may be firmly fixed. The mystery of man is nothing other than that impossibility.

The Impossibility of Definition

INDEFINABILITY

There is no thought that does not tend toward the question of love. Although this is the case from the beginning to the end of existence, it is worth testifying that love remains indefinable by thought. The fullness of love is the same as emptiness of thought. To love is the same as to be mad. This is the case because comparison, measurement, and calculation—the essential attributes of reason—lose both their importance and their meaning in love.

In all the descriptions and accounts of love, there is no definition that would make its essence known to reason. Whatever the factors defining love, they do not contribute to knowledge of it. It remains simultaneously in itself and in the self that feels it. And it is not exhaustible in any single one of its experiences. Thirst for it cannot be slaked even by love itself, but without being intoxicated by it, a person cannot be disclosed in his or her most beautiful uprightness, nor see in any one of the countless multitude of levels through which he or she passes from that perfection to ultimate formlessness. All discourse about love is the attribution of power to reason. It is so because love cannot be separated from being. Even so the indefinability of love is the way in which it eludes all power outside itself:

> You should know that things can be divided into two sorts. One
> sort can be defined, and the other cannot be defined. Those who

know and speak about love agree that it is one of the things that cannot be defined. A person recognizes it when it abides within himself and when it is his own attribute. He does not know what it is, but he does not deny its existence.[1]

Thought stimulates Reality in its totality and divergence. It is what raises a person above the level of an animal. Thought can be abandoned to itself, but cannot deny itself. Together with it is also the will, which directs it toward objects and holds it to them, but thought will sooner or later elude the will. Thus, thought moves constantly between closeness and distance, similarity and difference, gathering and scattering, unifying and sundering, letting go and encompassing.

Thought is enduring in the variability of its direction. It is sometimes here and sometimes there, but never at rest. Thus, it reflects Reality in its constant approaching and retreating, so demonstrating that Reality cannot be encompassed by thought. But, thought recognizes phenomena in their relation to one another. This comparison is what enables it to vary and determine the Flow and the rhythm in which things exist—originate, endure, and disappear—in space and time. It is possible to add to this existence of theirs descriptions in which individual phenomena are "captured" in an image of the law of their existence. It is through such laws that phenomena as such acquire an image in knowledge. A person then becomes a "separate" observer who knows what phenomena are and how they should be.

In knowledge, which is based on measuring and establishing models of phenomena, human presence is presented as exclusion from phenomena themselves. A person is reduced to immaterial observation. But, as soon as he is included, as soon as he achieves a relationship with himself, the world and God, his separateness is impossible. As soon as will, love, and knowledge are seen with their beginning or end in thought, thought becomes insufficient for their experience and revelation. And perhaps thought is entirely incapable of this undertaking. However, a person lives in the impossibility of a final answer. The power of speech, which nothing can exhaust, makes him what he is—a form that is open toward infinity, and, thus, also indefinable in terms of anything other than infinity.

Where there is life, there is also will. But, there is no will without love of the phenomena toward which the self is directed as toward its inner or outer center. And wherever there is love, there must also be knowledge and they—that love and that knowledge—are inseparable. The first without the second leads a human being to madness, while the second without the first takes away a person's freedom and openness toward infinity. But when will, love, and knowledge are harmonized in the self, then its center is revealed as a unity that gives meaning even to unappeasable thought.

Thought is not possible in oneness, but not without it either. The world belongs to thought and it to the world. Thought is possible only where there is multiplicity. But multiplicity is always duality—far and near, different and similar, merciful and angry, spiritual and material, and so on. Duality is the nature of everything in existence. Thus, the oneness, which is indivisible and distant, loves to be known. Manifestation is its aim. The totality of existence is the possibility of oneness whose love of revelation does not permit everything in it to remain unrevealed.

But revelation is descending and divergent. It does not deny oneness, but becomes its manifestation through signs in the outer world and in the human inner being. Every phenomenon is "rooted" in the inexhaustible possibilities of oneness and its love of making itself manifest. And everything that is made manifest strives toward oneness. Love moves, thus, out of oneness toward divergence and multiplicity, and out of all of that toward oneness. Knowledge bears witness to the divergence that emerged from love. And all divergence strives toward unity, and, thus, once again toward love. There is no phenomenon that does not seek to return to oneness. And that is its love. Thus, the divergence between phenomena in the world points to a oneness toward which each phenomenon strives as the "place" of its beginning and end. The love of a mother for her child is her witness of oneness, which, after its disclosure in unity, is revealed in multiplicity. The love of a husband for his wife is the confirmation of a multiplicity that wishes to be witnessed in the revelation of oneness.

Knowledge is the aim of love that comes from indivisible oneness, but oneness too is its aim that comes from divergence in existence. Oneness sees itself through multiplicity. And the other way around, multiplicity sees itself through oneness. They are two aspects of one and the same essence.

UPRIGHTNESS

Truth for a person means his existence through what he is. The human self is thus identified with its essence. But, thought is incapable of surpassing ontological objectification and fundamental duality. This is because thought is divergent in its essence. In relation to Reality, it is like the color white: it is not visible without light and cannot itself illuminate anything. In it one may clearly distinguish the divergence of existence into being and knowing. If this duality is to be overcome, being must become knowing, but knowing must also become being.

If existence itself is observed in its dual divergence, then it is necessary to be rather than to think, because thought indicates a direction but does not reach an aim. It does not encompass the whole human being, so its encompassing of Reality is even more limited.

This duality may be resolved in the following demand: to know only what is—God; to be only what is known—the Self. The attainment of that aim is deliverance or liberation from duality. And that includes the testimony that there is no identity other than the Self. Salvation is, therefore, in the self and attainable in its acknowledgment that there is nothing apart from the Self. Thus, the self is directed from itself to itself. It finds itself divided.

In a man there are, therefore, two identities present. They are not reducible to a common measure. Toward one another they are either nothing or infinity. Their aspirations are quite contradictory. But, there exists a "contact" or "connection" between them. On one side is the self of existence or the *anima*. It is woven of external and internal chance factors, among which memories and desires predominate. On the other side is the *spiritus*, or pure Intellect, whose identity is rooted in fullness. That Self or that pure Intellect sees the first self as a shell or something external and alien to the Self, which is the One and Only. And that Self is both transcendent and immanent.

Those two sides of the human identity, or those two identities in the human being, are indisputable. Of the first it is possible to say that it strives toward happiness and survival in happiness. And the visibility and justification of such an aim cannot be denied. But neither can it be denied that pure Intellect, which is one of the two sides of the human self, strives toward its source. The riddle about mankind is nothing other than the question of resolving this duality, which is outlined in the Exordium by the demand that the Self makes of the self:

> Guide us to the straight path,
> the path of those whom You have favoured,
> not of those who have incurred Your wrath,
> nor of those who have gone astray.[2]

This utterance contains the beginning of all human potential—orientation toward the Almighty, which is rooted in eternity and infinity, orientation contrary to what is facing nothingness; but also orientation that rejects existence without connection to the perpendicular line up-down.

If all the height and extent of the heavens, and all the depth and extent of the oceans, are looked upon, their meaning is nothing other than a sign placed before a person about that line. With it every phenomenon is forever before the Lord's Face. The division of the self into *anima* and *spiritus* enables it to let its belonging to the world of phenomena be seen from above, by the superindividual self, and the human self to maintain tension and change in which the last word is that of the *spiritus,* derived from the *Spiritus Sanctus.*

The human being is thus positioned on three levels—body, soul, and spirit. The soul is witness to the body, and the spirit to the soul. The human self cannot be identified with the body given that in its inner being the soul opens up as a world of feeling and imagining. The Center of this is the Intellect, through which the transcendence and immanence of the One and Only Self are revealed in a person. "The soul," says Frithjof Schuon, "is the inner witness of the body, as the spirit is the inner witness of the soul."[3] A person, therefore, has two directions—one toward the outer world, which he or she touches and experiences through the senses, and the other toward the inner being, in which he or she "contacts" the Intellect as its greatest potential. Between these two extremes of existence of person is one and the same infinity, which is shown and affirmed in a countless multitude of external phenomena and inner states and possibilities of the self.

To say "I" means to admit the experience of a border with the world of magnificent and unencompassable horizons, but also with the depth or height of one's own inner being: however far a person reaches—in either of these two directions—the question about the border between him or her and Difference remains unanswered. Difference passes through and surpasses everything. It is revealed in the other as the essence behind the form and as received beauty. Its attraction surpasses thinking. It wants the whole person. Thinking retreats in that attraction of Difference revealed in beauty.

At the border, every human "I" feels and knows itself to be denied and imprisoned. And as long as it remains so, the border will not let it go. In all its thinking about itself and the world, the "I" confirms and preserves this border, for the "I" cannot exist without it. Hence the human "I" longs and yearns for what lies beyond that border that is, release from duality. The "I" wants more than all its thinking can give it. The "I" is bigger than anything within these borders. This is why all its rational abilities cannot satisfy it. It wants more. This is why it longs to cross every border by bearing witness that there is no peace but Peace, and that there is no mercy but Mercy. Nothing that is partial and bounded can satisfy the "I" in its quest for itself.

Knowing this confinement within the whole of itself, the self strives to approach the Self and fulfill itself in It. And that means undertaking to resolve the duality of "I" and "you." In it the "I" recognizes itself in "you." But unity is possible only if the "you" also reveals and bears witness to difference as fullness. The relation of "I" and "you" is transformed into the admission of full otherness, which, by means of its oneness, passes through and surpasses all multiplicity.

Male and Female

It is possible to speak about love only through its effects or the traces that are accessible to remembrance and reason. The traces are simply the reflection of one in the other, while the essence eludes those traces that are revealed as incomprehension and madness. And the weighing up the speaker undertakes demands that those remains be differentiated and sifted: what is not madness is retained, while the rest is retracted and rejected.

All discourse about love is simply the interpretation of its traces and their transference to the other side of the current of love, where it exists as on a distant periphery. Whatever can be said about love is not love itself. And that is the reason incomprehension and madness are its real traces in the definable world. Whoever loves has a beloved who is veiled. But the lover seeks full revelation and identification with the beloved. When the veil completely disappears, there is no longer any duality.

It is said that when Samnûn the lover spoke of love, oil lamps began to come and go right and left.[4] People said to him: "Say something about love." He replied: "I know no one on the face of the earth to whom it is easy to speak of love," whereupon a bird came and perched opposite him. He said: "If such exists, then that is he." And he began to speak of love, and the bird beat the ground with its beak until it bled, and died.[5]

This discourse is pressed into an image whose essence eludes reason. It seems that to understand it requires knowledge that sees the borders and the changeableness of everything that is within them. It may be found in different approaches. That is why speaking about love is coherent both as witness of madness and as a harmonious endeavor to delineate the rhythm within the indefinable. Love reaches us as the reflection of speaking about mankind, the world, and God. When it is in that sequence, it is man's love for them—mankind, the world, and God. But, in duality there are two directions—giving and taking.

The totality of existence may be understood also as the presence of two elements—male and female. Those elements encompass one another in full harmony. Their unity produces or creates everything that exists. The relationship of those two elements is, from the perspective of oneness, constant change. Thus the totality of existence, of all worlds, changes at every moment, like a river. "Change" is the Flow through which the heavens and the earth, and everything in between them, are created again and again. Male and female are the initiators of that change and signs of all the movement in the world. That mutuality of oneness and the Flow of days is contained in the statement:

> Say: "God is One,
>   the Eternal God.[6]
> He begot none, nor was He begotten,
>   None is equal to Him."[7]

All phenomena form part of the Flow. No single one of their "suspended" states is not the Flow, but nor is anything outside it. The Flow is indefinable, but everything that is in it bears witness to it. Aspiration toward it means denying the seeming independence of its separate phenomena. In it and with it individuality outside it disappears: a bird alights on a branch, endeavors to pass through it and show its innerness in the Flow and with it. Its opposition to the branch through which it tries to pass, for the sake of the Flow in which everything exists, opens it whereupon it shows its innerness on the branch and its outerness "dies." But, this is always a mutuality of action and passivity. Those two elements are present in the worlds as the totality of existence, but also in every detail within them. Through their presence they cause the transformation and alteration of everything at every moment.

Everything is thus in duality, as He says in his Teaching: "And all things We have made in pairs";[8] "God created the sexes, the male and the female."[9] Every phenomenon in the world is paired with another. Some are the elements of creation: the pen and the tablet, the sky and the earth, the spirit and the body. Those dualities are the divergence of one and the same. They retain complete dependence of the one on the other. The relationship between them builds the harmony of existence. One is the need of the other: "They are a comfort to you, as you are to them."[10]

Speaking about love presumes the acceptance of God's commandment that His image should not be carved. All a man can attain in his turning toward God is always only an image. But that image is never God. Of mankind it is expected, and it is his lot, to cleanse his core of every image, so that it should be open for the One who created mankind in His Image.

Through this constant cleansing of his core by rejecting and destroying every achieved image a man constantly approaches the beloved. Not one approach can satisfy him. He contrives constantly to see himself as beautiful through his beloved and thus become beloved by his beloved. Not one of his states is anything other than an instant of that striving in which he dies, in order to be born in a new instant, but still more beautiful and closer to the beloved. The approaching is endless until it becomes a full free Flow in which a new and more beautiful image arrives at every moment as a new revival, and the previous one ebbs away as dying and forgetting.

This is the case because everything vanishes apart from the face of the beloved. As long as the "I" of the lover exists, the beloved remains far away. But the aim is to die, so that the redemption of that death should be none other than the beloved.

THOUGHT

Thought remains forever caught in the tension between the elements of duality. It knows only duality and functions only within it. But, duality is nothing other than the proclamation and confirmation of oneness. Thought deals with what is comparable and similar. But oneness is neither comparable nor similar. In addition, it is present in everything that is duality, and that means in the totality of existence. Consequently, to think means to compare. And that is possible only in a world of multiplicity, where phenomena are forms in movement.

The comparable has its space and time. But, more than that, the comparable has both a visible and a hidden side. The visible side makes it closer to the observer, but also more distant from its origin. But, every phenomenon has, along with limitations in space and time, also its quality. Thus, phenomena proclaim through their place, time, and quality what lies behind. And behind each phenomenon, and behind all of them together, is oneness—one and the same reality, which is both present and absent in everything.

Thought can bring one to the border, where comparability ends or begins. Where comparability comes to an end, thought ends too. But a person cannot reconcile him- or herself, in the full meaning of that concept, to anything apart from the perfection that surpasses and passes every limit, and that means also every form. This is the case because the person is not reducible only to thought. The question of identification with the Almighty, as the name of happiness and survival, is the core of the human drama. Thought takes man to the limit, whether the most remote one, oriented toward infinity and eternity, or the closer one, oriented toward an infinite point and eternal moment. But man wants that proximity. No single border is enough for him, since he would be enclosed by it and reduced to the limited world of thought. He can be made real only in the Reality which, as the one and only, is present in everything.

The human "why" is not exhaustible in the totality of existence. It wants Reality itself as its source and spring. If this highest human wish is denied, both the world and mankind become a prison with no way out. Only God can be the guarantee against such a prison. If thought has a purpose, if it becomes meaning, then God is its foundation. Every granting of meaning that can have a positive effect on human existence comes from that foundation, or descends from that suspended "point."

But, it is impossible to discuss God through positive phenomena, without discussing the world. This is the case since those positive concepts are God's names, which are understood through comparison and similarity. Even the names of distance and incomparability can be understood only out of their presence in the world. It is impossible to understand the Creator without creation, lordship without slavery, one who understands without what is understood, and so on. Without these "places" of the proclamation of God's names their meaning is unfathomable. What produces effects of every kind, on every level and in every presence, is God. And what receives effects of every kind, on every level and in every presence, is the world. Thus, to say "God" is to say "the world." And the other way around. Or, to say "one" is to say "two." And the other way around. One demands the other. If oneness is infinitely close to everything, then it entails multiplicity as its need. If multiplicity is incomparable with oneness, then that means that it is only its confirmation and that there is nothing without it.

"God is," says the Prophet, "and nothing is with Him."[11] Thus, when God says, "I am the hidden treasure!" that means that He is incomparable and infinitely distant. But when He says, "And I love to be known!" that means that His oneness requires and realizes duality or multiplicity.

Love and knowledge are thus two sides of one and the same. The beloved is known, the known is beloved. In oneness are all possibilities, but indivisible and unrevealed. Just as the hiddenness of fullness demands or loves oneness as its confirmation, so oneness too loves its revelation in countless multiplicity. Only the secret that oneness confirms and that is proclaimed thus by multiplicity is the Treasure of all that can attain existence, without anything's being added or taken away. This mutuality of the secret, oneness and multiplicity, in the descending and, opposite, ascending direction, starting from mankind toward collected multiplicity, oneness and the secret, is love.

Oneness is fullness. And that is why all possibilities are contained within it. In it, they are indivisible, but, since all possibilities are there, among them is also nononeness. And that means that Oneness can show itself in countless multiplicity. Fullness is goodness, which commits itself to radiating and creating. And whatever is created is also separate. Oneness is in everything, so knowledge of it is the striving and energy of return to it or unification with it. Reality is only oneness, so multiplicity is only its manifestation or its other way.

Thinking confirms itself as breath, voice, or speech—in the cry of a newborn child or the last breath of the dying. Voice and speech are a kind of action, and an act is, it seems, the most obvious confirmation of thinking. Thought resides in reason, which is the existence of the Intellect on a human level. The Intellect takes its light directly from God. "God has created nothing better than the intelligence," says the Prophet, "nothing more perfect, nothing more beautiful; the blessings that God grants are due to it (since it determines freedom of choice); understanding comes from it, and the wrath of God strikes him who despises it."[12]

Intelligence contains all that reason can accept, but whenever it reaches here, the level of reason, it is the image of a higher model. And when it descends, from on high, from thinking, into speech or deed, sacrifice takes place: everything in speech and action acquires an additional limitation.

The Intellect is the first fruit of creation and the apex of Divine revelation. It is the source of the descent or dissipation of the hidden into the world of limitless multiplicity of phenomena in which God's names are revealed. They are divided and scattered in the world. This descent reaches its ultimate limit in man, in whose form is gathered, revealed, and concentrated the totality of existence. From man comes the return or ascent to the origin of creation.

In order that it should be known, God's love brings about creation. He too reflects Himself through mankind. His love is that observation of Himself through another similar to what He is. And human love is the same. By raising up or making manifest his original nature man wishes to see through God. It is only in that love of Him toward him and of him toward Him that fullness may be realized, for only man knows the names, all of them.[13]

Every self makes manifest the Self, but in a separate way and with the possibility of turning toward nonself. Goodness in the self is the irreplaceable potential for its remembrance, which can be shrouded in forgetfulness, but never destroyed. Remembrance of oneness spurs every being toward overcoming duality and toward unity. Through this remembrance, the self remains open to knowledge as its realization. Refusal of that separateness and the energy through which the self is turned toward that center are nothing other than the love of oneness for multiplicity and multiplicity for oneness.

When one says "to think about love," in human nature one recognizes a level that it is not possible to identify through either will or knowledge. To speak about love means to translate it into thought and seek love's image in thought, then, afterward, in speech as a kind of action. Thought is capable of concerning itself with every object, moving around it—thinking about it. But, to love something is not to move around it; it is to be in direct contact with it—loving it, as distinct from thinking about it. More penetrating thinking about a subject means also the greater separation of mankind from it. And to love more means to be closer to the beloved and more integrated into it. Thought is possible only with reason, while loving almost does not care for the help and cooperation of thought.

LOVING AND LONGING

In what has been said so far, there appears a mysterious linguistic knot: the topic here is thinking about love, which imposes a strange overlapping of semantic fields in the center of which are the verbs "to want," "to love," and "to long."[14] When the words "to love someone" are spoken, that means that between the self as lover and the other as beloved there exists a connection, which is "loving." That connection for which the verbal noun "loving" is appropriate is called decisively "love." If the verbal base of the noun "longing" is analyzed, it is clear that it involves a relationship between the self who longs and the longed-for, the verb itself implying that the self achieves full closeness with the other, which on the first level of meaning represents touching of lips, when the act of speech, as the first confirmation of thought, becomes extinguished in the closeness of the lover and the beloved, when the relationship of subject-object or duality disappears. In this it is possible to recognize that the will is orientation toward the object of devotion, but that it cannot reach its aim, regardless of how much that longing and that loving cooperate in overcoming and surpassing separateness.

In the semantic difference between longing and loving, as in their related verbs "to love" and "to long," it is possible to glimpse the relationship of those two contents of being. If the semantic complex around the core "long" and the verb "to long" is analyzed, it is possible to affirm that it is not separable from meanings such as closeness and similarity, dearness and tenderness, touching and caressing, gentleness and beauty, and such like. In all these relationships may be discerned separation and the desire for unity. But, what the lover is unified with is not a determinable and stable object although all the signs in the world and being can speak of it. Although it appears to lovers that what they love is a phenomenon or a person from which or from whom they are separate and to which they draw near, no attainment can bring them the appeasement that would be constancy.

The object of devotion may be personified, but it is always more than that in which it is revealed. Whenever the beloved is seen in a person, striving to approach that person testifies to the fact that what appears to be the aim escapes the devoted just as the horizon cannot be reached by any journey. There is nothing that can satisfy the lover as long as he is divided from the beloved. Where there is will there is also fear. Will turns toward what can be loved, for which memory longs in the deepest center of the self. Considering that the self is in separation from the Self, it is in constant fear of oblivion or hurtling headlong toward non-Self.

What is designated as "will" is not, contrary to simple logic, the relationship of the lover and the beloved. That concept does not cover the fullness of this connection. Only one level is appropriate to it, or only one degree, of that relationship in duality, equally as the relationship of the one who wants and the one who is wanted is not wholly equivalent to the concept of "wanting." The difference between wanting and love is will. Thus, will includes wanting, but it is more than that. While love includes will but is more than that. To think about love means to reduce it to will in thought or to translate it from one level of the human character to another.

When love is revealed as the attraction between the lover and the beloved, in which its real aim cannot be determined, the form toward which the lover is directed, in order for the will to be expressed as the content of love, must be specified and recognizable. But, what the will is directed toward cannot be the determinable aim of love. It is just one of the stops on the limitless path of drawing near to oneness.

And there are three levels of that character or that content—will, love, and knowledge. In another kind of expression, these are three possibilities—submission or rebellion, belief or denial, and holiness or profaneness. When the will of the self is opposed by greatness and power, and anger and punishment, it is transformed into fear. And that fear drives the self to withdrawal or attack. With this return to greatness and power fear is admission or denial, while will is only a trace of the inner serenity that has crept into the depths of the self. Such fear confirms or denies greatness and power.

In flight, the self contracts and recoils. And when fear moves the self to the decision to attack everything that is not Self or fullness, so as to find refuge in Him, it expands violently. Both contraction and expansion approach a border or extreme. The borders of the skin, then the senses and consciousness, impose the question of what is "behind." Visible phenomena bear witness to their invisible root. They cannot be reached by either the senses or reason. They demand and impose passing beyond the borders, which is possible in faith—the attraction of what is the other side of a visible phenomenon, the need for everything that has descended to ascend, for everything created to return to the Creator. In the face of the certainty of the invisible side there occurs a relaxation in which serenity floods the being. Phenomena are shown in perfect order and confirm oneness. But, not everything that reveals itself may be stopped or grasped. Although that complete peace of oneness is quite close, it ceaselessly flows between inwardness and outwardness, the first and the last. Its serene restlessness once again moves the self out of its relaxation.

In front of man lies a world of countless multiplicity where one and the same essence lies behind every form. The recognition of that countless multiplicity of forms, of which no single one denies that one and the same essence, demands and imposes the division of the unreal and the real or the non-Self from the Self. Phenomena and their forms are nothing if they do not show the Real, for there is no Reality other than the Real. Acceptance of the Real means listening to its speech and accepting its commands. Although its essence is not visible, there is nothing that does not reveal it. To know it means to be it. And to be it means to know it. Phenomena in the world are nothing other than its confirmation. And that is the reason the visible world has its more real level on its invisible side.

The question "Do you not see the submissiveness of everything in the world?" confirms that both the Sun and the Moon, mountains and stars, trees and animals subordinate their will entirely to His will. They are thus, both individually and together, the visible side of His love of being known. By eliminating their own will, as a necessity of being separate, phenomena in the world reveal His love. The possibility of the human self to have its will is revealed in the duality of distance and closeness. When submission to Him is complete, then the will is identified with His. And that is attainment of complete closeness in which separateness is overcome. Here it is no longer possible to speak about the attainment of movement between the lover and the beloved. Simply, the self and the Self are united in a station of no-station, in the peace of the Flow and the Flow of peace.

What attracts as the proclamation of beauty, but remains indeterminable, makes the knowledge of different objects or different relations between the knower and the known only other veils of darkness and light on the face of oneness. Denial of this brings the self down into the world as sufficient unto itself. Thus the self "breaks away" from its upright prolongation to the first mind in which knowledge and the being are united. Then the will and love are in opposition.

EXTREMES

A person is situated between these extremes, given that he is in relation with fullness on the basis of faith, which is not possible without free will. And free will opens up for him the space between nothingness and fullness. The fact that he is within those borders, but that he can cross them and surpass them, does not mean anything other than that his heart is elementarily adaptable to every change in existence, and that as such it can rise above them through its connection with fullness, which is beyond every limitation and all change.

But the changeableness of the heart is resistance to the changeableness of the world. And that is revealed as the inevitability of suffering as the accompaniment of love, and pain as the companion to friendship. The stronger the will for attainment of the Highest, so the opposition of the lover to everything that lies between him and the beloved is the more cruel and merciless. In that thought systems disperse, since the opposition mentioned above includes the whole of the being. It reveals that wholeness cannot be reduced to any one of its contents. In this it is possible to know the reason the face and the heart are the two key phenomena in speaking about love.

The face is what is seen, that in which the inner being is disclosed. It is both divergence and unitedness. There is nothing that so clearly bears witness to duality and its surpassing. Duality united in the face, in which the looker sees himself, shines with beauty. And that relaxes the looker, directing him from thinking, which is dispersal and tension, toward the center in which totality is united. The face "descends" into the heart of the observer. In it thinking is surpassed. That is the connection of totality with its revelation in beauty. It does not remain in confrontation with the face. Relaxation and embracing what is revealed as beauty suppress thought. But they are transformed into attraction, which is directed by the will rooted in the heart as the center of the entire being. Rational explanations and their coldness are in conflict with that will and are most frequently powerless before it.

The difference between love and knowledge becomes clearer: knowledge is the relationship of the one who realizes and the one who is realized, during which they may be distant and without mutual attraction; as soon as the object of knowledge is revealed as a face, that is as beauty, the connection descends from reason toward the totality of the being and love floods knowledge. That path from knowledge to love is not a necessity. Another direction is also possible: beauty is directly knowable and it is as such loved and attractive, and it spurs and demands knowledge in which the separation of the knower and the known could be removed through unity. In both cases love is revealed as inseparable from beauty as the proclamation of the Essence and surpassing of separation.

Beauty, closeness, and similarity stand in contrast to greatness, distance, and difference. Thus, it is possible to say that the entirety of existence diverges between the extremes of greatness and beauty. That duality is in complete harmony and confirms oneness. It is conceivable as the divergence of the whole of existence between the two hands of the Creator. Its sheer dividedness reflects the intensity of the opposition between distance and incomparability on the one hand, and tenderness, closeness, and similarity on the other. Greatness, distance, and incomparability give rise to fear, while tenderness, closeness, and similarity give rise to and maintain joy. The self is afraid of His anger and hopes for His satisfaction. The extremes of this duality, greatness and love, are revealed in the self, which encompasses also the proclamation that God created Adam with His own two hands.[15]

This duality may also be expressed through the Secret, the Hidden, and the Invisible, which are the equivalent of the Essence and the Visible, which are the equivalent of the world. The Visible confirms the Invisible, just as duality confirms oneness. Such divergence shows that greatness and beauty are in God's names. But this divergence is expressible both as God and as everything other than God. And only on the basis of that divergence is it possible to discuss the two different realities, even if, in the extreme, the other is just the shadow and appearance that reveal the Essence.

God is made manifest through creation. But the world as His creation is not He, but nor is it anything apart from Him. Given that He is one, the world is a countless multiplicity that is reducible to duality as sufficient confirmation of oneness. And that is the reason for God's testimony about the creation of all things in pairs. Only He is the One and Only. His creation confirms Him and reveals that oneness through its duality. Creation is not possible without oneness, although it is duality.

Every phenomenon has its opposite. In the countless multiplicity of phenomena no single one is or can be the center. To realize or surpass that dividedness means "to take refuge" in oneness.[16] All phenomena that reveal oneness are arranged into invisibility or visibility, or between the heavens and the earth. These phenomena have originated in the relationship of giving and receiving, but they are forever in it. Thus, the invisible and the visible, and the heavens and the earth, are in the nature of every phenomenon. They are in them and with them even when they are "between" them. Their aim is in Reality and with it. A man may, on the basis of free will, deny that harmony that is with Reality, but he cannot surpass it. It comes back to him one way or another.

SECOND DOOR

Will

A person appears to himself by means of what his will offers him. And it can turn him both toward the body and toward the spirit, toward the earth and toward heaven. But this illusion of the sufficiency of his will, as separate from the Will in which lies all potential, distances him from the trust that his madness reveals as love, and his calculation as madness.

> We offered Our trust to the heavens, to the earth,
> and to the mountains, but they refused the burden
> and were afraid to receive it. Man undertook to bear it,
>   but he has proved a sinner and a fool.[1]

Refusal of the offered trust is the only reasonable response of the created to the Creator, if it is based on calculation. That means accepting being only the recipient of the Almighty, being only His slave. But, such a response denies the love whose reasons lie in neither weakness nor power. Neither weakness nor threat can be an obstacle to love. Both the endurance of violence and enterprise, despite their evident madness, remain unknown and despised in relation to the beauty of the Face in which the lover sees himself. No arguments of the reason can participate in that surpassing of duality through the testimony that there is no face other than the Face nor beauty other than Beauty.

And not only that. Trust is the relation of the faithful, or those who have faith. And faith is love that wishes to know the beloved. It is also knowledge that wishes to love the known. The fact that God says, "We have offered," or, "Let us make man in our image, after our likeness: and let them have dominion,"[2] confirms that the hidden is the oneness or completeness of the Self. But this oneness is revealed and confirmed by countless multiplicity, in which every sign discloses oneness. Thus, the Self discloses Itself through this multiplicity, but without losing anything of its oneness. For Him/Her it is the same to say "I" and "We," for He/She is made manifest in the totality of creation.

Trust between the supreme I and every other I means that the love of the first is revealed in the second and that knowledge of the second is reshaped into love for the first. Only man unites the totality of knowledge about the Creator. With that knowledge, his love overcomes every individual phenomenon, recognizing in it the mark of the Creator. Faith is, therefore, love of knowledge and knowledge of the loved.

The will is always revealed in denial or action. It means restraining oneself and saying "no" to evil and what is unclear, or doing what is good. In that way a person directs himself toward goodness as the essential character of his self. This direction presupposes a divergence in the self. For, if there were no such divergence, direction would not be possible either. What is divergent, therefore, consists of what is higher and lower, or closer to the origin and more distant from it.

This establishes a debate in the self. Its higher character reproaches what is lower. And as long as there is "breath in the body" there is no end to that reproach. It is reflected in the irreconcilability of reason: the nonabatement of the inner debate corresponds to the immeasurability of relations between phenomena in the outside world. Both are reflected in the will, which is in a state of ceaseless reorientation. Its "teaching" presupposes consciousness of its aim. It follows the inexhaustible possibility of comparison within which reason functions along with all the reflections of that insoluble war between the higher and the lower in the self.

The task of every spiritual act is to confirm that the divergence of the self into its lower and higher horizon bears witness to the axis of existence between the truth and nothingness. Orientation toward the truth is the essence of every action, although truth surpasses it. The role of such an act is to instruct and accustom the will in its orientation toward the truth, in its restraint from everything apart from it and in its giving of everything a person has. For, nothing other than the truth is sufficient, and nothing that a man has received is his. Although truth is in everything and with everything, it is the ultimate judge of everything. The reverse is not valid.

But human freedom, which makes him a being to whom God as fullness offers trust, enables him at every moment to revoke every choice of direction. Without the possibility of turning from the Purpose to nothingness, a person is not in trust with God. All that a person has is nothing other than a gift he has received out of fullness. But, as nothing can be fullness other than fullness itself, a person is essentially a poor man who through his essential emptiness bears witness to his own condition as debtor, for his possibility of stating "there is no fullness other than Fullness" is at the same time his initial orientation toward the resolution of duality in his self.

This is one's initial orientation, but it springs from free will. The division of truth from untruth takes place through this will, but judgment is always above it. And that is the reason every divergence includes also fear. Where there is the human will there is also fear. When that will disappears and becomes entirely Will, fear is transformed into certainty. And this is the highest possibility of trust.

Although trust includes divergence, its outcome is unity. And the self wants nothing other than that unity in the Self. The self therefore draws near to the Self in a constant need to know It. The self is moved and directed that way by love. Knowledge as the aim and love as the inner impulse are faith. They make real the essential oneness in a person, but as return or unity. God is faithful, since His alliance with man would not exclude love and knowledge without man's freedom to choose within the range from nothingness to fullness.

As long as a person is in a state of dividedness—and that means in a form with borders—return and unity are his aim. The closer he is to these, the reality with which he is created is the more clearly revealed in him. His self disappears increasingly in order to reveal the Self. A person wishes to see himself through the other, and in the act of realization he "positions" and "regulates" himself, in order to be seen and heard through the self of the other, to be what he is in the most beautiful uprightness of his original createdness. This "positioning" and "regulation" are nothing other than his acceptance of action assigned to him by truth, which is infinitely close to him. When the aim is achieved—and that means when trust is actualized—the self discovers that "I am for him hearing, sight, and tongue. Through Me he hears, through Me he sees, and through Me he speaks."[3] Then the Prophet's statement is actualized: "He who knows himself knows his Lord."[4]

MERCY AND WRATH

And will is just that possibility of resistance to evil—whether through attacking it, or fleeing from it—and of doing good—through giving or denial. If phenomena in the self and the horizons are "with truth," the presence of evil in mankind and the world is divergence along the above-mentioned axis from fullness to nothingness as impossibility. All phenomena "with truth" deny the primary nature of evil, although a person cannot either avoid it or surpass it until he is in his entirety returned to nonduality. Thus, since evil is not primary, neither is it predictable. Not one of its forms takes on a final and enduring expression. It is only through evil that orientation toward the Origin demands and stimulates the openness of the self with which the transition away from phenomena as revelation of the hidden and toward the hidden itself is disclosed as freedom.

But, disclosure is not and cannot be complete, for no outwardness is possible without inwardness. Overcoming that duality is not possible without violence. Regardless of the extent of that violence, the duality of outwardness and inwardness cannot be overcome.

The will always has an object. Out of the human inner being it is directed toward the object of the outer world, or the object that comes into being through the division of the very self. In that process sameness is always present in the source of the will and difference in its object. The essence includes in itself every possibility in its undivided aspect. The possibility of being revealed imposes duality on it. And that is its desire. In the root of that desire is the will. Its strength is revealed as love. Out of it springs the trinity of essence, love, and revelation. But revelation is possible only in duality. Where there is love, there is also duality, and the other way around—duality is only the possibility of revealing oneness, so its overcoming is the love that is present in each participant of that duality.

There is no phenomenon that is without its "spouse." It is in that division and the longing of one for the other that mercy and love are "situated": "And of His signs is that He created for you, of yourselves, spouses, that you might repose in them, and He has set between you and love and mercy. Surely in that are signs for people who consider."[5]

"Of yourselves" means that part of the original whole is distanced from it, or that the "spouse" is that alienated part. The longing of the self to achieve once again its original oneness is its need for its spouse. For its part, unity is return from alienation to the original homeland or wholeness. And there is no satisfaction that could be greater than that renewed unity of what was separated.

Duality is in a state of constant change. And that means it is in a state of possible balance and imbalance. In the outer world that inexhaustible changing is revealed as the divergence between the heavens and the earth. Everything on earth receives everything that is in heaven. And this is a relationship of action and passivity, giving and receiving. Since man is the sum of the entire outer world, his division is between the spirit and the soul, and between the male and the female. Balancing that duality, in which complete harmony is complete humanity, depends only on oneness, or the heart as its complete revelation.

The duality of spirit and soul presumes turning toward perfection in which the whole receives its missing part, which, thus, returns to its homeland. When that connectedness is denied or broken, then the part is seen as the whole, and the whole as a part. Then the self is subordinated to the lower or the soul that induces evil, and the will acts "downhill," against the attractive power of the spirit, which is with the creative commandment. That inversion of the sequence spirit-soul into the relationship of soul to body is revealed as wrath or as the opposite of mercy, which is approached through contrary movement, through the soul, "which reproaches" and thus attains Peace and Mercy.

Teaching and directing the will in an act that is revealed by truth itself are not possible in relation to evil, since it is not primary and the self does not find rest in it. Such teaching is connected with the "most beautiful example," such as every prophet—who in the outer world is the center of its wholeness—and with the Intellect—which is in the human inner being and through which the link with the Almighty is maintained. But, concentration on truth, whether through a prophet or through the Intellect, is tested and "corrected" by the fact that every phenomenon evades both evil, as nothingness toward fullness, and good, which cannot be exhausted in any state of being closed, nor, therefore, in any form.

The will cannot find its root in evil. Every experience with evil will direct the will toward the other and the different. It is not possible to satisfy the will in the light of reason, as the presence of Intellect in the totality of the self, although the will can neither pass reason by nor surpass it. It is only with the will's transformation into the abandonment of everything, apart from what is revealed in forms as beauty, that the will leads toward belief as love and knowledge.

The outer world offers itself persistently and unremittingly to the self as an object that is impossible to avoid. It is divided into the duality of sky and earth. Everything that exists is in them and between them. The material, visible, or sensible world is the manifestation and witness of the immaterial, invisible, and insensible. These two sides are closely intertwined, even if they are understood as opposites, which is the condition of their recognition. The heavens are not comprehensible without the earth, nor the earth without the heavens. Thus, the heavens are a sign of the invisible, insensible, and spiritual, and the earth of the visible, sensible, and corporeal. That duality is matched by commandment and creation, or mercy and wrath.

But, each of these divergences is in Reality and with it. In the last analysis, duality is the revelation of oneness as mercy, which encompasses everything.[6] In creation there is nothing that is fullness, but neither is there anything that is not with it. There is no complete light, but neither is there complete darkness. Thus, the world and its phenomena are bathed in light and permeated with mercy, which are essential fullness, which darkness and wrath are not and cannot be.

CORRUPTION

Given the apparent luxury of the myriad phenomena in the outer world and man's inner confusion after the fall, ascent toward the most beautiful uprightness, in which mankind is made, means turning away from everything that is evil and unclear. In such a turning away, stimulated by the original nature of the self with its memory of oneness, lies orientation of the non-Self toward the Self. And it is not only orientation. After knowing in the place and moment, the self sets off toward the Real. The self is recognized as a guest in the world of limitation and moves toward oneness as its refuge. And nowhere other than in unity can it achieve full satisfaction. That is why the negative expression of the will is closer to sanctity.

Man renews or discloses himself in his original perfection by finding and accepting what is forbidden, for through losing that he has fallen into a state of darkness in his inner being:

> To Adam He said: "Dwell with your wife in Paradise,
> and eat of any fruit you please; but never approach this tree
> or you shall both become transgressors."
> But Satan tempted them, so that he might reveal to them
> their shameful parts, which they had never seen before.[7]

As is seen in the Teaching and known from the whole of human experience, the human will can be opposed to the Divine.[8] The opposition of those two wills—the human as limited and contingent and the Divine as limitless and complete—is nothing other than denial of the truth that there is no self other than the Self. That denial brings about a turning of the contingent self toward knowledge of creation without the Creator and the reduction of being to its contingent revelation. In that way, the human essence declines toward the "lowest plains" of existence.

The will may be redirected from movement down that slope toward the opposite—movement toward truth and patience. Turning toward that ascent means also seeking refuge with the Lord from evil, and from that which is revealed in phenomena and their changes, in people and in the corrupted consciousness. Every turning away from the self is nothing other than acceptance of the insolubility of division and the primary nature of non-Self. Thus good and evil are equated and become two principles.

The fact that a person may have a will that is not Divine, and that he or she may love what God does not love, directs one toward the only knowledge through which, in its divergent and uniting aspect, a person may surpass or resolve duality. Abstention in the face of the forbidden and acceptance that knowledge of That Which Is includes also acceptance of division means that, as long as there is human will, there must also be a clear division between the self and the Self. And that is renunciation of all otherness apart from God, separation from all revelation for the sake of that toward which it is directed, being sober in the face of all signs in the horizons and being fearful before God. This is how one must overcome desire, passionate attachment, and the acceptance of gods other than God, which means peripheral things and their contents apart from their center or true reality.

Evidence of turning toward gods other than God—whether they are passions or the external justification of individual or collective powers—is involvement in the unclean, depravity, suffering, and death. This is connected with hatred of God and fighting against Him and

His Emissary. The inevitable consequence of this is retribution, which acts within the selves of such rebels. It implies surrendering to their self or cruel preoccupation with the self. Their enmity toward ethical injunctions causes them to lose insight into all moral values; and their consequent mutual disagreement and "corruption" cause endless conflict among them for the sake of gains and power in this world: they kill one another in large numbers, torture and maim one another in large numbers. The consequences of this are that whole communities are swept away or, as it is stressed in the Teaching, "banished from the land."[9]

This is all caused by the will that has lost contact with the constant changes of all that exists. For it, phenomena and names have acquired relations apart from the essential creation. In that way both phenomena and names are in the wrong places. Or, the veil placed between man and the Creator has been torn aside, and, consequently, in the human inner being the lower and the higher have become apparently identical: with equal decisiveness it is possible to affirm that the world springs from both nothingness and fullness.

There is no element before which the will is going to abandon itself to the attraction of beauty. If that potential of the self is considered in its divergence along the axis spirit-soul, and mind-reason, it is not difficult to recognize that the soul falls or rises showing will in its opposition or submission. As long as divergence exists, knowledge is contingent and incomplete. But divergence comes from love. And there is knowledge as long as there is divergence. In oneness it is the hidden. Thus, love seeks knowledge, while knowledge leads to unity for the sake of love:

But when I became a man,
I put away childish things.
For now we see through a glass, darkly;
but then, face to face:
now I know in part; but then shall I know
even as also I am known.[10]

To be "a man" means to be distant from the beginning but with awareness of it, with knowledge of return but still in separation. No knowledge in that is true, but neither can it be without truth. Unity is full knowledge through being face to Face, when the self sees the Self and nothing else, for there is nothing else to be seen.

CERTAINTY

Opposed to impurity, corruption, suffering, and death are Purity, Sanctity, Happiness, and Immortality. That separation from the world that has been deprived of its "true reality" becomes a foretaste of death. Since "now" and "death" are the only certainties in human existence, withdrawal from everything that is between them for the sake of connection with them means the victory of life over dying. That is concentration on the Moment, Peace, and fear. Two other certainties correspond to "now" and "death"—God and the Day of Reckoning. Thus, these four names, in which lies certainty, proclaim oneness in existence, and hence one and the same certainty is revealed in different ways.

God is now, so deliverance from the fragmentation of human existence is possible only through the harmonization of the will with the Will. Death is the loss of everything that is received and reduction to a right toward the world, which springs from complete powerlessness. It is also a debt to God. Thus, death is a meeting with the Death-giver Who is alive and outside every death. Unity with Him is salvation. Given that He is fullness, and as such Living, there can be no complete death. It is possible to say the same for each one of His attributes, such as Mercy, Purity, and so on.

But, since the world is what is not God, nothing in it is fullness although nothing in it is without it. And that is the sense of the pronouncement: there is no god other than God; there is no fullness other than Fullness; there is no reality other than Reality; there is no knowledge other than Knowledge; there is no sanctity other than Sanctity; there is no mercy other than Mercy; there is no beauty other than Beauty; there is no love other than Love, and so on.

But the world—the totality of the material and the spiritual, the earthly, and the heavenly—offers divergence within the signs about the Self. Each sign has two sides, one toward the Self as secret and the other toward the world in which that secret is revealed. This division of every sign into its two sides is not sharp. Between them is a transition in which there are both light and dark, knowledge and ignorance, Reality and non-Reality. That is why it is possible to say of every illumination that it is dark in relation to the higher level of existence, of all knowledge that it is ignorance in relation to the higher proximity of fullness, of every Reality that it is unreal in relation to the higher proximity of Complete Reality.

The reverse is also possible, depending on the adoption of the downward direction from the first intelligence toward man. The contingency of everything in existence raises the question of conviction, lack of doubt, and certainty in knowledge. Knowledge that has any level of certainty may be acquired only through the observation of the mutuality between fullness and phenomena. Those mutualities are determined by the wide range of qualities that are encompassed by God's names and attributes. Those names and attributes give mankind the potential for conditionally complete orientation toward the realization of the true nature of phenomena.

The divergence indicated by the duality of the heavens and the earth, the invisible and the visible, the spirit and matter, as also the multitude of people, has its root in original oneness—"the heavens and the earth were but one solid mass"[11] and "It was He who created you from a single being."[12] Thus, the totality of existence corresponds to God's creative injunction willingly, since the beginning of everything lies in the proximity and clarity of His nature.[13] It is the same with man. He at first responds to God's question "Am I not your Lord?" with the affirmation "We bear witness that You are!"[14] These responses, which are both voluntary and from the center of the Creator's commandment, remain a source of certainty to which a man turns out of the total duality of existence. The original closeness is guarded by divergence and distance. They strive toward it as toward their deepest nature.

Oneness directs the mass regardless of its divergence and dispersal. To say "Creator" means to assume createdness. But, since the Creator is always what He is, the question arises whether creation after His coming into existence still remains merely eternal potential, for a Creator is not possible without creating, and without creation's having a beginning and an end. Therefore, everything in existence is in a state of potential. Creation as potential does not elude the eternity of the Creator. But, before His many and indivisible names became revealed in the phenomena of countless multiplicity, they were that "before" without which there is nothing real. When they are in existence, all phenomena are like the creation of dualities—certainty and potential. The first is made manifest in the other, which confirms it as such but is everything that certainty is not. Thus, every duality confirms certainty, which is the "partition" between the two seas of the duality of manifestation.

Where names and phenomena are indivisible existence begins. But everything also returns there. Since in this source and confluence of everything there is no divergence, it is not even conceivable. If knowledge is the relation between the one who understands and what is understood, there, in that indivisibility or mystery, knowledge is not annulled. There it is the same as being.

But the manifestation of the Creator demands creation in which certainty remains in indivisibility, whether in its source, or in its confluence. And the love of indivisibility toward itself transforms potential into existence. Here too love is actualized, but it is not liberated from its presence in oneness. Out of existence, love "draws" toward the oneness of knowledge and being. It is an enduring link with certainty and its revelation in the world as the limitless multiplicity of phenomena.

THE HEART

The will must both deny and affirm: if it must deny objects toward which the self strives, in view of their deceptiveness, which is revealed in changeability, it must also affirm them, in view of its freedom of choice. Denial comes from freedom. Through it the self establishes itself in its divergence: an inclination to evil, reprimand, or the constant remembrance of several possibilities and, finally, the attainment of peace in which human and Divine will are reconciled through the same satisfaction in the actualization of the truth that there is no will other than the Will.

Free turning toward the Will includes effort and the struggle of the higher levels of the self against the lower ones for the sake of ascent or becoming upright. Through it the self opposes the provocations and lures of the world and itself. The contingent being endeavors to rise up and achieve a feeling of sufficiency and that means nothing other than its solidification—or, as it is said in the Teaching, "the petrification of the heart" or "the sickness of the heart"—which is brought about by harnessing the will and forcing it to act from above toward below.

Thus, the self is divided in its verticality between the body, as solidification toward nothingness, and the spirit, as the highest level in existence.

The horizons of the outer world reveal the divergence of the names of infinity and eternity to their concentration in one point and moment. Everything that is dispersed in the horizons of the outer world is gathered together in man, in his body, which corresponds, in the outer world, to the earth, his soul, which corresponds to what is in between, and his spirit, which corresponds to the heavens. The tension between these possibilities determines human destiny. The spirit, or the mind, illuminates the totality of the self, but light is mediated through the heart. The state of the human soul is determined by the degree of impediment to that mediation. The soul will be turned toward Peace, which is in the spirit and mind, or the passions, which are in the soul and body.

In view of the fact that the whole dispersal of phenomena in the outer world, which correspond to the countless multiplicity of names, is gathered together in man, his center includes a countless multiplicity of vistas. And that is the reason the heart is the "place" of turning, returning, change, flow, etc. Just as looking at the globe through the bodily eye offers a countless multiplicity of images, with a change of position, bearing witness thus to the oneness of space, the heart too is revealed as oneness in multiplicity. This makes it capable of receiving oneness as the potential of a multitude of names, of being the receiver of their dispersal into phenomena as signs, and of taking from multiplicity signs and names and of knowing the oneness in them.

The heart is, thus, at the same time, both gathering and divergence. It is turned toward both oneness and multiplicity. And that means also toward greatness and distance and toward closeness and beauty. When divergence takes place within it, love as the source of revelation is transferred into phenomena. Thus transferred, it is the enduring mover toward renewed attainment of oneness. In the heart lies the gathering or unity of knowledge and love as faith. Outside it, they are divided, but they are also the revelation of what is first and last, the inner and the outer.

The heart is the child of the relationship between the spirit and the soul. In the multitude of possibilities in that relationship, the soul is revealed as the power of turning the being away from the light of the mind and instruction, while the spirit draws it toward God. From this point of view, the relationship between the spirit and soul is revealed as one of tension and conflict. But if the soul subordinates itself to the light of the spirit, the relationship will be harmonized and balanced. That harmony of the spirit and soul is comparable to the marriage of the First Mind to the General Soul.

The offspring of that happy, joyful marriage of the spirit and the soul is the heart, which is a child in the form of the Merciful. Thus, the totality of signs in the horizons and selves reaches into that heart. It is both the beginning and the end of everything that is in the self and its passage toward everything in the outer world. In it are all names, as both potential and manifestation. Both separation and unity are in it and through it. Given that only the Essence is one and the same, everything in existence is in a state of constant change of relations between action and reception. There is no single instant nor single physical point in existence that remains the same. The heart too is an "interface" in which the change of that duality in existence is brought into equilibrium. In it both oneness and multiplicity are constantly revealed.

It is worth repeating that the heart is a link toward the uncreated and uncreatable center of man. In a mysterious way, it is the highest level of the human being. It is immersed in the Intellect, and thus in "contact" with its root. In view of the fact that the self is in a state of constant change, the heart is the potential of supposing, receiving and returning to it. In that way the heart is above every change, but is also its origin in the totality of the self. And that is the sense of the statement: "The hearts of all the children of Adam are like a single heart between two fingers of the All-Merciful. He turns it wherever He desires."[15]

Its "sickness" or "hardness" closes it off from the Higher and steers it in the opposite direction, toward nothingness, or separation from that ray that "links" the highest with every phenomenon, where every direction offered by phenomena and the connection of reason with them is left without a reliable measure of their quality and the extent of their harmony with the purpose of human existence.

The virtues of opposing and battling against such orientation include decision, keeping watch, and endurance. That is a spiritual act, and it is in turn conditioned by them, not in its unique actuality, but in its relationship with duration, which demands repetition, rhythm, the transmutation of time into instantaneity; the spiritual act is, on its own plan, a participation in Omnipotence, in the Divine Liberty, in the pure and eternal Act. What has to be actively conquered is natural and habitual passivity toward the world and toward the images and impulsions of the soul; spiritual laziness, inattention, dreaming, all have to be overcome; what gives victory is the Divine Presence, which is "incarnate," as it were, in the sacred act—prayer in all its forms— and thus regenerates the individual substance.[16]

THE INTELLECT

The nature of the Intellect is not to identify itself passively and blindly with the phenomena it recognizes. Its aim is the reduction of phenomena to their essence, "to know ultimately That which knows; by the same stroke, the sage—precisely because his subjectivity is determined by the Intellect—will tend 'to be That which is' and 'to enjoy That which enjoys.'"[17] The trinity of existence, Consciousness, and Blessedness is revealed in divergence although it is just one Self. That Self speaks in the self:

> In the Name of God, the Compassionate, the Merciful,
> Praise be to God, Lord of the Universe,
> The Compassionate, the Merciful,
> Sovereign of the Day of Judgement!

These words, which are a discourse between the Self and the self, include the resolution of the subject-object duality. The Self descends into the self, in order to make possible also the ascent by which the self rises to the Self. It is only in this way that the self recognizes in the worlds, as an elemental and clear object, just as in itself, the reason for the affirmation: "We are in thrall to Thee and we praise Thee." Directing itself along that path toward the oneness of the subject and the object, the self submits voluntarily to one will. In that way, it comes before the Essence, which is veiled. But, disclosing it, the self discloses itself, in order to free itself from the semblance of duality: for, to know oneself is nothing other than the knowledge of the One. In that being before the Veiled, which becomes disclosure, the self travels along the road toward encounter and unity.

That passage is ascent if the aim is shown as Beauty, which directs the will toward Beauty and impels the will to drive or draw the self despite its laziness and weight. "The most beautiful uprightness" is also primary perfection. Nonacceptance of the untouchability of the veil disturbed the balance of primary being at the apex of existence, so the self is exposed to the division of two opposing wills—one that draws it toward the plain of existence and another that reminds him of his primary state or the apex of existence:

> Have We not given him two eyes,
>   a tongue, and two lips,
> and shown him the two paths?
> Yet he would not scale the Height.
> Would that you knew what the Height is.
>   It is the freeing of a bondsman;
>   the feeding, in the day of famine,
> of an orphaned relation or a needy man in
>   distress; to have faith
>   and to enjoin fortitude and mercy.[18]

Two eyes placed in a straight line and two lips, whose separation indicates verticality, bear witness to a language or discourse that reaches into the world of space and time out of the core or oneness. The two paths are upward and a return to the core, or downward and distance from primary perfection. The first is reflected in humility and generosity, and the second in arrogance and miserliness.

The will, which is active on the first path, maintaining the domination of the higher over the lower, grants itself disappearance into the complete will, which is nothing other than belief—love and knowledge. But the will that is abandoned to descending the steep slope is revealed to itself as power and sufficiency. In the slope it seems that the will has no power over man, nor that anyone ever sees it. The enslaved and hungry, orphans, and the suffering reveal nothing on that path about the self that is opposite them. They are not the state of self of the one who bears witness to them, but merely one of the phenomena of the outer world. The self in descending the steep slope becomes more and more confined in the sufficiency of its will. Neither patience nor Mercy has any essential meaning for it.

In the "hidden treasure," love of revelation is the potential of undivided phenomena to attain existence. Attaining existence means "clothing" or "enveloping" preexistential archetypes in one of the multiplicity of phenomena of the world. Coming into being, creation or revelation is separation and being clothed in form. Each of the phenomena in the outside world, or "in the horizons," is a sign of the oneness and indivisibility of the "hidden treasure." Everything that is divided and revealed "in the horizons" is gathered together in the self. Both—the world and the self—indicate Him. They are first in the Intellect, which is the beginning and the return of every phenomenon.

The Intellect distinguishes the hidden and discloses the unknown. The Intellect is the first consequence of love. The Intellect and love are a duality in which the first draws out the second, and the other way around. Since God is the Light, the Intellect is inseparable from illumination. Its light removes the darkness. Thus, the Intellect enables phenomena to proclaim oneness by distancing themselves from it and clothing themselves in forms, and also to return to it by removing their clothing and drawing near to it. As such, all phenomena are in duality—spirit and body, heavens and earth, light and darkness. Dualities are the manifestation of oneness. That is the nature of the Intellect of which the Prophet says:

> The intellect is a fetter against ignorance. The soul is like the worst of beasts. If it does not have intellect, it wanders bewildered, since the intellect is a fetter against ignorance.
>
> God created the intellect and said to it, "Turn away from Me," so it looked away. Then He said, "Turn toward Me," so it

turned toward Him. Then He said, "By My might and majesty, I have created no creature greater than you nor more obedient than you. Through you I shall begin and through you I shall bring back. What is for you shall be rewarded, and what is against you shall be punished." [19]

THIRD DOOR

Love

DIVERGENCE

The will is expressed as endeavor and action in the opposite direction from the one in which the self is drawn and confined by the lower levels of the soul. Such a will is good. Its orientation toward good confirms evil as opposition. It is not possible to understand that good will without its opposite. The freedom of the will includes also the possibility of its agreeing to the opposite of such orientation. Since the human self is divided between fullness and nothingness, its realization involves turning to and enduring on the Righteous path. Contrasted to that is the opposite action. The extreme of the first is wrath, and of the second Peace.

If human perfection is considered in its earthly manifestation, then it is the balancing of those opposites in connection with heavenly glory: "Glory to God in the highest, and on earth peace, good will toward men!" say the heavenly prophets, announcing the birth of the Anointed One.[1] The appearance of the embodied Word in that pronouncement is connected with objective reality, with the world in the heights that makes manifest God's glory; opposite those heights, at the other end of the perpendicular, on the surface of the earth, is man in relation to other people, where that mutuality may be direct, without the heights that are proclaimed in every sign or through it.

Out of mutuality with the heights springs the recognition of signs in the horizons as the discourse of truth. And these are the presence

and discovery of beauty in phenomena. The Face of God is proclaimed in that of man. That is why the heavenly is recognized in the
earthly, and the Divine in the human. The human core is the apex of
both the heavenly and the earthly, the passing through and surpassing
of phenomena and openness to the One. The objective world becomes
an inscription that is transformed in the reality of the Self. The love of
Being Known is revelation. Here good will is seeing oneself through
another. Orientation toward the perfection of the Anointed One has
three stages—the heights and the vertical, which are proclaimed by
the heavens; lowness and the horizontal, represented by the earth; and
centeredness and inclusion, gathered together through good will
toward men.

In this divergence the heights correspond to the Spirit. Directedness toward them is striving for Peace as the primary reality of the
self. It is only in that striving that divergence may be resolved as
the realization of the self. When it is resolved, there is no duality
of the spirit and soul. But the self in the world means also the presence
of that divergence. Good will is opposed to the soul, which is inclined
to evil and incites to it and does not permit it to become its mistress.[2]

The spirit attracts the soul, since at every lower level the soul feels
a stranger and finds in a return to its source movement toward the
home of fullness. Thus it marries itself to the higher, which takes it
and accepts as a condition of its fulfillment. The strength of the will,
through denial and separation, opposes the attraction of the world.
And when the will expresses an affirmative attitude to the testimony
that there is no god other than God and that the Praiser is God's Emissary through prayer, giving to others, restraining from taking or fast-
ing, and undertaking the sacred journey toward the given aim, then
too the will's submission to commands, which has the form of acceptance, indicates refusal of that toward which it is drawn by its corporeal nature and the undirectedness of reason.[3] The greater the power
of that denial of gods—whether they are passions, accustomed closeness, blind habits, or confinement in systems of thought—the more

evident it becomes that the will itself, or the submission that it stimulates and maintains, is not sufficient to enable the territory in the soul in which it reproaches itself to be crossed, and for it to give itself up to the attractive power of Peace.

And Peace is the highest potential of the self. It cannot be satisfied by anything else. And God is perfect Peace,[4] and He too has satisfaction in showing the freedom of the self in the actualized truth that there is no will other than the Will, and that human purpose, as its source, is that perfect Peace. Human subordination is nothing other than the endeavor to reach the field of attraction of Peace and to escape the power that acts in the opposite direction.[5] That attraction, which acts in the higher level of the soul, is love. Original human nature bears forever also an unchangeable "imprint" of the love of original creation, love that is revealed as beauty.

The separation of the unreal from the real and acceptance of the real strengthens the will in its identity with the Will. That is revelation of the will of the self as surrendered to the pleasure of the Flow by which it is attracted to the Will of the Self. God says in the sacred saying, "I was a Hidden Treasure, so I loved to be known. Hence I created the creatures, so that I should be known."[6] That original Divine love is the uncreated and uncreatable essence of every revelation—of both the cosmos and mankind. It is that "innate tendency" of the human self that makes possible consciousness of "the true faith,"[7] as it is proclaimed in the Teaching:

Therefore, stand firm in your devotion to the true Faith,
the upright Faith, which God created for mankind to embrace.
God's Creation cannot be changed. This is surely
the right faith, although most men may not know it.[8]

Faith includes separateness. And when one speaks of the Self as fullness and self as contingent, then the relationship between them is separateness in which both sides love. The Self loves the self, for in that way all His potential is realized. They each look at one another over the other, in which process reality is their secret unity.

"The True Faith"

It is possible to understand that injunction to stand firm in one's devotion to "the true faith" also as directing man toward his deepest human nature: a person is nothing other than a debt to the Creator and complete, original purity. The debt is accepted in trust and its repayment is inevitable. A man's good will affirms his original nature, which is debt and purity. Through instruction that will is directed toward the Face or Beauty and discloses its inner being as love. "Therefore religion is the same as love, and love is the same as religion," says Imam Bakir.[9]

In original purity faith is constant and complete. Given that faith is the same as love, the human core or the uncreated and uncreatable Divine breath in man is His love of beauty. Thus, concentration on that breath in man leads to surpassing and passing through the world for the sake of Divine love. "A believer can taste the sweetness of God's love," says Imam Sadiq, "if he abstains from the world. He will thus succeed. Then he will attain God's love. He will be considered to be insane by those who love the world, but in fact the sweetness of God's love has made him attend to nothing but God."[10]

Since Peace is the highest human potential, the desire of Peace for another is the same as loving him.[11]

Love is rooted in the will, but also free from it. The transformation of the will into love, as man's striving for Peace, includes the recognition of the verticality that begins from each of his states and leads toward fullness. The possibility of such a recognition of man's being in the center of the surface with a multitude of paths is transformed into intention: the self is revealed on the edge and is directed toward the center. Such an intention is submission. The perfect intention is perfect submission and harmony with God's Will.

The search for absolution and the turning away from the self to the Self is acceptance of the truth, and is achieved through its image, given that God made man in His image. Submission is, therefore, revelation of the source and confluence in the image, and so it is the essence of every act of directing the will toward harmonization with the Will. Intention and submission are inseparable from desire and will. "The Fall is equivalent to a turning away of the will from God," writes Whitall N. Perry. "Man is redeemed when his will is again concentrated, definitively, upon God." [12]

But, being a man means to be separate. In the horizons or the totality of the outer world, one hears, sees, smells, and feels otherness. The human self is opposed to it. Beauty is revealed in the self as a subject and in the world as an object. It is in them, but also outside them. Man knows it directly as his deepest and highest nature, but not also as reducible to separateness. Although beauty is always revealed in phenomena and never in the same way, beauty is one and the same and inseparable from love.

Where there is beauty, there is love, and the other way around. The attraction of beauty, which is nothing other than love, bears witness to man's original purity, perfection as his core, and the endurance of his debt to beauty. "God is beautiful and loves Beauty!" [13] Since beauty is made manifest in the other, its attraction is nothing other than the action of original human nature or the revelation of the self itself.

The mention of love usually directs one to the connection between male and female, the giving or taking of a wife, marriage—whose core is *eros*—conception, and birth. Marriage does not surpass separateness and human distance from the pure core and fullness as its aim, but without directedness toward oneness—and original perfection is that and nothing less—every attraction in the field of love is suffering. Love is the aim that confirms sense and suffering, which it transforms into a way of bearing witness to its fullness in the world of phenomena.

Love is in the depths of man even as water is in the depths of the earth, and man suffers from not being able to enjoy this infinity which he bears in himself and for which he is made.

It is necessary to dig deep into the soil of the soul through layers of aridity and bitterness in order to find love and to live on it.

The depths of love are inaccessible to man in his state of hardness, but reveal themselves externally through the language of art and also through that of nature. In sacred art and in virgin nature the soul can taste, by analogical anticipation, something of the love which lies dormant in it and for which it has only a nostalgia without experience.[14]

RELAXATION

The will leads up the steep slope to the Height, so the self is in a state of tension.[15] The sense or awareness that through denial and letting go the range of the consciousness or vision becomes broader and that for the most exalted position the will is insufficient—all this stimulates the self toward relaxation, to abandoning itself to the gentleness that reaches down from the higher horizons behind phenomena through which the thought floats freely. In that state of contemplation the separate signs in the horizons and the selves are recognized.[16]

Rays shine through the veils on the Face of God, which is always and everywhere before man, so the illumination of the soul's higher levels is more clearly revealed. There are more and more signs revealing Divine Beauty and His love of beauty.[17] Thus, the first level of love is the presence of beauty. In it relaxation is revealed as serenity, harmony, and balance. Although the possibilities of phenomena are numerous and various, they are not in disorder or conflict: everything moves along given paths.[18]

In such relaxation, the knots of the soul are loosened, and sensuality, lack of concentration, and anxiety are removed. Serenity springs from Divine Peace, which is the Compassion of infinite Love. And love always and everywhere in its root has serenity, relaxation, and the balance of possibilities.

Beauty bears within itself every element of happiness, whence its character of peace, plenitude, satisfaction; now beauty is on our very being, we live by its substance.[19]

That serene relaxation makes it possible to discern in it horizons and selves. Then it becomes clear that the eye that looks cannot ever see itself.[20] For, even when it is seen in a mirror, however clear the image is, one must conclude that it is not the eye itself. It is merely an image, and completely reversed at that. When the eye looks at itself in the mirror, its actual right side becomes the left side of the reflected face. And relaxation and serenity on the first level of love make possible the understanding that every human consciousness is only the reflection of Reality and its looking at Itself.

And the complete mirror is the Intelligence, the first to have been created and through which all else has its sense only in Completeness. Through it God looks at Himself. It is the uncreated and uncreatable core of the self, whose "eye of the heart" is nothing other than the Eye of Truth. In it the Praiser, Praise, and the Praised are one and the same: the complete meeting with the Praiser is the same as the meeting with the Praised. Man's relaxed serenity is abandonment to that Completeness. It is resting in the center, abandonment to Sight and Peace, for there is nothing that God does not know, while man can never know everything, nor hide anything of his knowledge.

Since God is the identity of knowing and being, and man becomes this only when his will is extinguished in that of God, existence is always also fear, for ignorance is its inseparable content regardless of the level of a man's exaltation or the minuteness of the remaining difference between being and knowledge. Man is always with fear, and God never. That is why the sincerity of fear opens one toward God's Mercy.

No single human state means also complete lostness, given that God's Mercy embraces everything and that it surpasses His wrath.[21] Thus, the state of relaxed serenity in which the attraction of Peace can act is granted Mercy: the self lives in the certainty that everything that it loves must be sought in God and from Him.

POVERTY

Opposed to the certainty that everything may be received from God, and that, consequently, it is necessary to turn and abandon oneself to Him, is the denial of everything else, since human openness cannot be satisfied by anyone or anything other than God. The required turning toward God and away from everything that He is not means flight from everything and a search for refuge in God. The will is a necessary, but not also a sufficient condition for that turning. Attainment is always also gain: the door at which one knocks is opened by none other than God;[22] what is found is given by none other than Him;[23] and the response to the summoner is none other than His.[24] It is thus because only His Mercy embraces everything.

Serenity and the embracing of the spacious view of reality in the human consciousness do not exclude the contingent self and its insecurity. From this state of relaxation and from the level it has attained, the self endeavors to step out into what is embraced by its serenity. And that means emerging from oneself for that is, after all, only an image of God's Face, which is revealed in Its full Beauty. Here duality is manifested as melancholy, sorrow, and pain in the self. The Beloved is, nevertheless, both near and far. Near because there is no one either equal or similar to Him, far because the lover is separated from the Beloved: he can call Him and speak to Him, but the lover is merely the image of the Beloved. That stimulates the ardor in the will to come still closer and abandon itself to the Beloved. Relaxation before the Beauty of the Beloved, looking toward Him and listening to Him soften the heart, but do not exclude the will.

Duality is revealed as unsustainable separateness. It stimulates listening and expectation: "Surely in the remembrance of God all hearts are comforted."[25] But everything that may be heard is also transient: "All things shall perish, except Himself."[26] "That is," writes Frithjof Schuon, "the melting of the heart in the divine warmth, its opening to Mercy, to essential Life, to infinite Love."[27] Openness in which God's Mercy is revealed strengthens zeal. It is thus because the tenderness of the heart in understanding that all signs in the horizons and the selves reveal Him transforms relaxation into new activity. In that relaxation sadness and weeping come together in the conviction that there is none other than Him, and that knowing Him is the only path to actualization. And that is not possible as long as there is a self outside the Self, which in its oneness both is and knows.

Out of this new activity a man directs himself toward those who in his experience before "the melting of the heart" were distant, other, like strangers and orphans, dead, and sick, for in their apparent powerlessness and distance the Beloved is revealed, and the way to follow Him is by turning toward them. In the luxury of the world, which manifests the veiled state of God's Face, His presence is disclosed in the neighbor and the stranger, the orphan and the beggar.

That veil remains in every human state. Man cannot remove it. In that inability one feels poor and weak. Gentleness and Mercy are begged from what is veiled. That is why the poor and weak are its image. Loving them is revelation of the self.[28] Weeping and tears indicate and bear witness to a state of inner activity—joy or sorrow, longing or disappointment. And when they are linked with phenomena, they bear witness in their depths to the Flow out of that human center and toward it. Meeting revelation and its transference of the Flow out of the center of existence and toward it stimulate man to humility and weeping: "They fall down upon their faces weeping; and as they listen, their humility increases."[29]

That turning from openness toward the signs in the horizons and the selves reveals the presence of Praise in everything created:

> He is God:
> there is no god but Him.
> Praise is His
> in the first world and in the last.
> His is the Judgement,
> and to Him shall you be recalled.[30]

Knowledge is possible only in divergence. Thus, love is the aspiration that unity should be attained out of divergence. The testimony that there is no god other than God is seeing oneness in multiplicity, and the aspiration that it be achieved as beauty to which love leads and that comes from it. And that too is knowledge of the Praise of oneness in every detail of its revelation.

Existence as the totality of phenomena in time and space bears witness to the first and last things, and to inwardness and outwardness. Every phenomenon has that duality of beginning and end. But since the full beginning and end are the same thing, the placing of a phenomenon in the duality of the beginning and end affirms oneness. Thus, the world bears witness also to the greatness of the totality of existence. But the fact that the world is a perfect balance of the beginning and the end means that it bears witness also to the qualities of the beauty of oneness. Every phenomenon, through its firstness, loves its lastness. Since every phenomenon has a form as outwardness, it is in such a relationship with itself and with the totality of existence that through its inwardness it endeavors to bears witness to oneness with its outwardness. And that is love.

The order of the world is maintained by the balance of the active and the passive principles. Although the world is what is not God, it does not deny His oneness. That oneness is confirmed by this duality of the active and the passive, the male and the female. And duality in relation to oneness is countless multiplicity, which is reducible to the two original sides—power and beauty, light and darkness. The Prophet sums this up in his pronouncement: "God has seventy thousand veils of light and darkness."[31]

The totality of existence is the relationship between those veils through which His most beautiful names are revealed. In the Divine

Treasure those names are indivisible potential. They are in their creation a descent or revelation in the countless multiplicity of phenomena, as the Almighty says: "We hold the store of every blessing and
send it down in appropriate measure."[32]

Everything, or each phenomenon, has a name that corresponds to
it. That name is in the Treasure, uncreated and inseparable—always
one and the same as everything else. When it is revealed in existence,
it remains one and the same. And that is the reason why "I" can say
of Itself "We" and why that "I" says, "We hold the store of every
blessing." Revelation in multiplicity is the love of that "I" for the Self
through all that has been created.

Thus, given the aforementioned duality, two views of the world are
possible. In the first what is emphasized is the incomparability, distance, and otherness of oneness. In the other view what are emphasized are the qualities of His similarity, closeness, and Mercy.

The incomparability of God with anything in the worlds means His
distance. To this correspond His names: Almighty, Unattainable,
Great, Exalted, Creator, King, Wrathful, Vengeful, etc. Those are the
names of highness or ferocity or righteousness or wrathfulness. Those
names emphasize greatness, power, authority, and maleness.

In order for the names to be brought into connection with the other
side of the duality from which they are inseparable and to which they
give and from which they receive, it is necessary to return to the question of the creation or revelation of the Hidden Treasure. For that it is
possible to take the image of the second letter of the Arabic alphabet
and the first letter of the Torah and Qur'an. That is a half circle with
a dot beneath it. As the second letter it can designate the totality of
creation, in its visible aspect. It corresponds to reflection upward or
"the spirit of God" moving "upon the face of the waters."[33]

Thus, that image is a circle, an invisible one that belongs to higher
reality, and another invisible one that corresponds to the world of phenomena lowered down in "appropriate measure." That is the image
of lowering that corresponds to division and revelation through which
the world enters into its multiplicity until in the human being it attains

its greatest divergence. That same image represents also ascent or returning through which the human being completes the circle. Creation goes from oneness toward multiplicity and back. At every level of that going down and rising up, reality is revealed with two faces. One face is closer to oneness, while the other is closer to multiplicity. One is proportionately less divided than the other. Thus each level is revealed as the simultaneity of the passive and the recipient, the light-bearing and the dark, the powerful and the beautiful, and the male and female principles. Depending on its direction, rising up or coming down, one and the same face is at one time active, and at another passive, at one time male and at another female.

God's names, such as Power and Ferocity, correspond in spiritual psychology to human states that are determined by phenomena such as confusion, fear, and shrinking. That is the reaction of the human self when confronted with power, ferocity, threat, death. That fear is imposed by incomparability and distance, while similarity and proximity bring intimacy.

BEAUTY

Nothing in the worlds is comparable to God. But, nothing in them has reality apart from Him. Thus, similarity is opposed to incomparability, since He is praised by every word in the worlds.[34] Incomparability and similarity are simultaneous, and they correspond to the "is/is not" of all existence.

Every phenomenon in existence has visibility and invisibility. In the visible, it diverges toward the horizons, in which it is revealed. In its invisible side it is closer to the higher and indivisible level, on which all phenomena are closer to the Hidden Treasure, which they reveal through their existence. That duality of the visible and invisible, the outer and inner, builds a chain of worlds. There is no single phenomenon without a border between those two seas in which it is plunged. At that border the visible and invisible, the outer and inner meet and unite in a mysterious way.

Duality is the revelation and confirmation of oneness. But when any phenomenon loses that connection or that contact, through which it is "with the truth," it becomes turned only toward nothingness. As such it has acquired in human understanding its distorted or corrupted image. And, given its original connection with the Hidden Treasure, every phenomenon is the revelation of beauty. In distortion and corruption it ceases to bear witness to Beauty, and is revealed as ugliness. Incomparability and similarity are the nature of every phenomenon. They are distorted when the duality that maintains them in connection with the Hidden Treasure is not understood as the affirmation of oneness.

To the above-mentioned similarity correspond the names: Beautiful, Close, Merciful, Most Merciful, Loving, Tender, Forgiving, Giving, etc. They are known as the names of beauty, tenderness, abundance, or Mercy. They are names of a receiving openness or a giving femaleness. They express subordination to the will of others, and therefore softness, acceptance, and receptivity. Opposite them and with them are the names of an initiating activeness and a searching maleness. As such they turn the self toward the outside or the world as everything that is outside the self, everything that is beyond the border of the individual. But He is with the selves, wherever they might be.[35] And this confirms that the border between the self and the outer world is an illusion, and the fact that there is no self apart from the Self confirms the similarity through which duality is denied.

The human response to those names of tenderness and closeness is intimacy, hope and expansion. And this is attained through love. Full unity is the aim of love. But being a phenomenon in the created world means also being in dividedness. The phenomenon seeks what is similar to itself, through which it may be seen in its reality. And that is its moving along paths in space and time. This confirms the fact that behind all these names there is one and the same essence. Love is the aspiration toward the oneness behind every phenomenon.

He who loves to know himself is revealed in the other in order to see himself through him. He both threatens and promises that other, for he does not recognize his aim apart from the revelation of himself through him, and at the same time he does not deny his oneness as fullness. Thus, that other whom he loves and who is beautiful for him is he/she—the self, which wishes to reveal itself to itself. But he/she is necessary to her/him only as he/she. The self wants nothing other than fullness. That is why his/her Mercy toward the one through whom he/she looks is original and all-encompassing. Unity is possible only in the fullness of that Mercy.

Separation and the pain that is inseparable from it are only states on the path of unity, which is nothing other than a return to one another or the affirmation of oneness, of which the Prophet says: "The good, all of it, is in Thy two hands, while evil does not go back to Thee."[36] The pain of separation ignites the fire of love:

Passion is the elixir that makes (things) new:
how (can there be) weariness where passion has arisen?
Oh, do not sigh heavily from weariness:
seek passion, seek passion, passion, passion![37]

No statement about love can avoid the questions of separation and unity. Love always contains the reality of proximity and distance. Although love is primarily connected with Divine love and tenderness, it demands also power and ferocity. Everything that is in existence reflects and bears witness, in its endless game of duality, to Divine Beauty and Divine Power. Collecting Rumi's statements about this, Annemarie Schimmel says: "God's twofold aspects are revealed in everything on earth. He is the Merciful and the Wrathful; His is *jamāl,* Beauty beyond all beauties, and *jalāl,* Majesty transcending all majesties."[38]

Love is always inward. It enables the self to know its deepest reality, its original indivisibility revealed in creation, as beauty. That revelation is immediate. Where the self finds beauty it recognizes that love which seeks that its original fullness be seen. That is why beauty has the power of attraction; it is love that is revealed in the other and that is satisfied only in actualization through unity. And it is not surprising that beauty and love have also semantic closeness with touching, contact, consent, and joining together.

The revelation of love is nothing other than the proclamation that multiplicity comes out of indivisible oneness and moves toward it. Love stimulates the self, while beauty attracts it. It is like this because the fullness of the self lies in the unrevealed mystery. Coming into being and returning, are, therefore, rooted in oneness, love, and beauty.

When the individual self in beauty, which is made manifest by an encounter with the other, recognizes "alien" property, it stimulates it to envy. Its eye becomes envious and that is why it is understandable that the Prophet seeks refuge in God from the "envious eye."[39] And that is why it is also understandable why the imam 'Ali the son of Husein prays:

Blind the eyes of our hearts
towards everything opposed to Thy love![40]

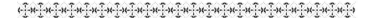

FOURTH DOOR

Toward Peace

"HE IS THE ALL-LOVING"

The revelation of perfect Peace means separation: the Revealed remains what He is—"I am"—and what makes Him manifest takes nothing from Him, nor does it add anything.[1] Everything that manifests Him remains in the original love of Him Who reveals Himself, and has its reality in its return, which is not postponed: both the present moment and death are its constant presences, its inseparability from Eternity and life. That Source is the same as the Confluence. And that is the potential perfection of every phenomenon. The aspiration toward it, or return, disclosing, and realization, is love. It is the oneness of the Source and the Confluence, for creation is in love: "I was a Hidden Treasure, so I loved to be known. Hence I created the creatures that I might be known."[2] "It is He who brings into being and then restores to life. Forgiving and benignant."[3]

Thus, the Self in His oneness confirms His hiddenness. And multiplicity and movement in what is created confirm the oneness and peace of that Self. Every detail of that multiplicity has its perfection only in its manifestation of oneness and peace. That is the love of everything for the Complete Being. Man contains the totality of creation. He forms its center, in which the self submits to the Creator through its free will. That is, according to the Teaching, man's original alliance with God:

Your Lord brought forth descendants
    from the loins of Adam's children,
and made them testify against themselves.
He said: "Am I not your Lord?"
They replied: "We bear witness that You are."
This he did, lest you should say on the Day of Resurrection:
"We had no knowledge of that," or: "Our forefathers were, indeed,
idolaters; but will You destroy us, their descendants, on account of
what the followers of falsehood did?"[4]

Existence in its totality and man as its complete sum attain original
realization by passing through degrees of appearance toward nonap-
pearance. These are oneness in multiplicity and attraction in rejection.
The Self is attractive and that means every sign of His revelation. But,
the Self is behind and in front of the phenomenon, and in it: "Whichever way you turn, there is the Face of God."[5]

The attraction of phenomena bears witness to their aspiration to
reveal the Self as their only perfection. That is the original witness, or
Divine love in revelation. It leads and sets in motion every phenomenon in its aspiration to draw nearer to the higher level of being. Such
a rising up or drawing near to oneness, which is stimulated and led by
love, is the relationship between the phenomenon and the One. All
phenomena, in their essential nature, praise the One.

The gathering of creation into the human core means that man
knows authentically the true names of all phenomena. They are the
Praiser, because they reveal perfection. And man's highest potential
is following the Praised, for in Him it is proclaimed that He is beautiful and that He loves Beauty. The harmonization of the self toward
that Beauty, or loving God, means complete openness, free flow or
tenderness of heart. "There would enter Paradise," said the Prophet,
"people whose hearts would be like the hearts of birds."[6] Free flow
and tenderness of heart mean that they are in direct relationship with
God. That is set forth in the legend about God's turning of the human
heart between His two fingers.[7]

But the Praiser's heart is freed of every image. It does not accept them, since no image is or can be God. The Praiser's heart is thus cleansed of everything. In it nothing can be constant, since it is only for God.

And that is why loving God is the limitless openness of the human heart toward Him, but through following the Praiser; and that is the way that God loves those followers.[8] That following of the Praiser from which God's love is inseparable determines the nature of the loved: "God loves those that turn to Him in penitence and strive to keep themselves clean."[9] "God loves the righteous,"[10] "the charitable,"[11] "the steadfast."[12] "The Merciful will cherish those who accepted the true faith and were charitable in their lifetime."[13]

DEBT AND LOVE

The relationship of man and God, in which they love one another, is the way of human existence in which his totality is included. Repentance and purification are maintained through the will or enduring remembrance of God. This is how the original connection between phenomena and their names is maintained: man knows them in his response to God's commandments. But reaching that is always also dependence on the Independent. Loss is the constant potential that confirms the accepted offer of belief that man will repay his debt for what he has received. The Confider speaks of the preservation of that relationship: "Believers, if any among you renounce the Faith, God will replace them by others who love Him and are loved by Him, who are humble toward the faithful and stern toward the unbelievers, zealous for God's cause and fearless of man's censure."[14]

That debt [faith, *Trans.*] has two essential contents—verticality, as the connection with God through the totality of existence, and humility, as being on one level of the multiplicity of revelation of oneness. Man's connection with the phenomena of one level of existence can also entail forgetfulness of the vertical. Then the attraction between details is revealed as the acceptance of a god other than God. That is no longer love as the relationship between the lover and the Beloved Who Is Oneness.

The rupture of the alliance or nonfulfilment of the debt turns man toward the love of phenomena that have ceased to be signs of perfection: such people love this life more than the world to come;[15] they worship idols, bestowing on them the adoration due to God;[16] they love riches with all their hearts.[17] That is choosing idols instead of God as a mark of mutual love in a life that is enclosed in the space and time of one level of existence.[18]

Names and phenomena are no longer connected through God's commandments. Phenomena can be given false names, and they associate with one another independently of their Origin and Purpose. Whenever those relations and connections are returned to the Ultimate, these alliances, the attribution of false names to phenomena for the sake of their association, will deny one another and fall apart in the repayment of their original debt: "On the Day of Resurrection you shall disown one another, and you shall curse one another."[19]

But that attraction is general. It includes also relations of individuality. Since man has accepted "the trust offered," his relation toward oneness includes also free will. The Face of God, which is in the veil of creation, both behind and before him, may be identical to phenomena that are attractive. This is revealed as the denial of the Face or as association with Him. Through these signs in the horizons and selves their nature is taken away and illusion adopted.

Every phenomenon individually, as all of them together, has a visible and an invisible side. The invisible side is turned toward the higher level of existence, while the visible one is turned toward the lower. That division in the turning toward the spiritual and the material is never complete, because phenomena, through their duality, reveal oneness. To differentiate in this, as in every other duality, the higher from the lower and the Real from the unreal means to recognize that every phenomenon is a stage that shows descent and ascent. The active principle descends from the sky in order to be accepted by the earth. But, every acceptance is at the same time also the aspiration of return to the Real. Return is the realization of original closeness to the Creator's command.

Love is the reason for creation. And knowledge is its aim. Therefore, love and knowledge are one and the same in the Creator's commandment. Division in creation is the precondition for understanding oneness through its revelation in multiplicity. The created submits to the Creator's will. Every duality in the totality of existence bears witness to the division that is the proclamation of the Creator and the created. That proclamation reflects and confirms the Creator's love.

The heavens and the earth are, also, the image of that relationship. Given its beauty and virtue, the earth is lovable. Heaven marries it not only for the sake of the debt, but also for the sake of satisfaction and pleasure. In this way the oneness, which is the original nature of both heaven and earth, is realized. Existence is separation, which does not eliminate the original oneness. Return is unity. It is the debt of existence toward oneness. The self loves oneness and that is why it returns to it.

Marriage of both men and women is return. It is the aim, the reason for which is love of oneness. Only with that love toward oneness and only with that return does the self become the crown of all creation. The subjection of everything the heavens and the earth contain to the human self is nothing other than the return of everything existing to oneness through man's love for it.[20]

The duality of the active and the receptive, and the spiritual and material, realizes its affirmation of oneness through the marriage of the first to the second. This is indicated by Ibn al-'Arabi's account of paternal-maternal mutuality in speech: "The speaker is a father, the listener is a mother, and speech is a marriage. What comes to exist from this within the understanding of the listener is a son."[21] Fatherhood and motherhood are a duality that confirms oneness. A good relationship with them is the highest human duty arising from the testimony of oneness.[22]

Reality is hidden, and its manifestation is potential. The marriage of reality with nonreality gives rise to existence as potential. That potential is the love of oneness for its revelation in multiplicity. A child, as the outcome of that love for its manifestation in the duality of fatherhood and motherhood, bears witness to the perfection of human nature, which is identical to the perfection of the full revelation of being. It is the place of revelation of perfect humanity in whose root is a harmonious marriage. That is the perfect balance of all the beautiful names and the manifestation of oneness in all signs, or "the station of no-station" given that in it nothing predominates: all is in the one and the one is in all.

INTOXICATION

Love for oneness is transformed, through the truculence and closedness of the heart, into different relations among details. Then the self, in its withholding and insensitivity, is placed in the center. It takes itself as the measure, and denies all other states, which demonstrate potential transformation in connection with oneness: "They desire nothing but your ruin. Their hatred is evident from what they utter with their mouths, but greater is the hatred which their breasts conceal."[23]

Such closedness toward Eternity and life is shown in the states of the self that God does not love—aggressors,[24] corruption and those who spread it,[25] the impious and the sinful,[26] the evil-doer,[27] the arrogant and boastful,[28] traitors,[29] criminals,[30] the profligate,[31] those who deny.[32] All these human states, which God does not love, do not exhaust and do not deny the original perfection and the possibility of its renewed discovery.

The original beauty of signs in the horizons and selves can be revealed as sufficient unto itself and independent of Him Whom they make manifest. Man's freedom is testified also in turning toward God's Face and away from Him. It constantly lies between oblivion and remembrance. Human perfection is tested also by the possible transformation of the love of God, which means seeing beauty in His every sign in the horizons and selves, into love of the signs themselves. Turning to God means the acceptance of the signs as such, since, without God, they are only deceits and illusions. "My love for good things has distracted me from the remembrance of my Lord; for now the sun has vanished behind the veil of darkness."[33]

The goods of the world are transient revelations. As such they make Him manifest in intransience. The denial of phenomena is nothing other than affirmation of Him Whom they make manifest: "You shall never be truly righteous until you give in alms what you dearly cherish."[34] "They love those who have sought refuge with them; they do not covet what they are given, but rather prize them above themselves, though they are in want."[35]

The signs in the horizons and selves are not and cannot be anything other than the proclamation of oneness. Every other content they have means denial of the harmony of names and phenomena. They cease to point toward Him Who loves to be known and they shut both the selves and the horizons. The relationship between them holds back beauty, but stimulates lustfulness: "Men are lured by the enjoyments of this life."[36] The reverse of that is the consciousness of the original debt and directedness toward the First and Last:

> Righteousness does not consist in whether you face toward
> the East or the West. The righteous man is he who believes in God
> and the Last Day, in the angels and the Book and the prophets;
> who, though he loves it dearly, gives away his wealth to kinsfolk,
> to orphans, to the destitute, to the traveller in need and to beggars,
> and for the redemption of captives; who attends to his prayers
> and renders the alms levy.[37]

When the order from the higher toward the lower, from the active to the receptive, from the male to the female, is reversed, then satisfaction in closeness or unity ceases to be a relationship with oneness. The mere place of revelation will be taken for the source of satisfaction. In that place where man has satisfaction there is no witness of Reality, which would be through one and the same testimony in which the giver and the receiver are united. And that testimony confirms that He is not limited by His revelation to the giver and/or receiver, neither individually nor together. Drawing near or unity remains without the knowledge of oneness in which details are engulfed in the satisfaction of union.

To take a wife means to receive the nonexistent part in the whole and to establish harmony of spirit and soul; to give oneself to a husband means to return to the whole or to confirm that only the harmonious duality of the active and the receptive makes oneness manifest. Thus, the Prophet says: "A person who marries achieves half his religion, so let him fear God in the other half."[38] Marriage is the condition for achieving the satisfaction of disclosure in sexual union. That union is complete and includes the participants absolutely. But, if they see themselves as the source of satisfaction, and not the oneness that is revealed to them and to which they are returning, half of the debt remains unattained and is transformed into intoxication.

When the male loves the female only for the sake of satisfaction that fulfills his natural need, he lacks knowledge of the aim of such a need. Marriage then becomes form without spirit. Although that form has spirit, it is not witnessed in the coming together of the male and the female, since the desired and expected satisfaction is without knowledge of where that satisfaction lies. In that case, the soul does not ascend to the Spirit to be satisfied and to satisfy in peace. Such a person loves satisfaction, but as the place where he finds it. The knowledge eludes him of what satisfies the soul and whom it satisfies. And only with that knowledge is perfection possible. Every satisfaction without that knowledge is intoxication. It is the admission of incomparability along with the denial of closeness, or the admission of closeness along with the denial of incomparability. Union as the aim of love is nothing other than intoxication if it is satisfaction without witness of the Real.

BALANCE

Creation as such is submissive to God. With man as God's viceregent it is a whole. Without man the submission of the worlds is complete and without freedom. With him it also has freedom: man can maintain his most beautiful uprightness in complete submission and out of free will. Thus he becomes a bridge between the worlds and God, a viceregent in the totality of existence for the sake of Divine revelation.

In Divine oneness all the names of phenomena exist as undivided potential. They are divided and scattered through the worlds. And here they are submissive to God: "Do you not see that those in the heavens and the earth, the sun and the moon and the stars, the mountains and the trees, the beasts, and countless men—all do homage to God?"[39] The expression "countless men" emphasizes that only man can be an exception. In that way, he is a special factor in the totality of creation. Thus, only his relationship with God is free. And that is a condition of trust in which they—God and man—faithfully swear to one another, God as fullness or affluence and man as emptiness or poverty.

What is scattered through the worlds is gathered together in man: he is the image of the Merciful. The scattered as a whole is the submissive or the serene (as *Islam*). Balance between everything is the way of existing in creation. Man accepts and adopts that way of his own free will. Thus he realizes the good in himself, his nature as the Divine image and createdness in the most beautiful uprightness. By doing this out of his own free will, he is faithful with the Faithful, oneness in which distance and incomparability—none is equal to Him;[40] nothing can be compared with Him[41]—are revealed in closeness and similarity. God is closer to man than his jugular vein;[42] He is with you wherever you are,[43] and whichever way you turn there is the Face of God.[44]

Thus, a man who prostrates himself lives together with all the phenomena in the heavens and on the earth. And that is his path. Along it multiplicity is revealed in oneness and oneness in multiplicity. From the viewpoint of Divine incomparability and nonsimilarity, all the phenomena of creation—both individually and as a whole—are submissive to Him. From the viewpoint of His closeness, the qualities of creation and the Creator's name are gathered together in man, and therefore only he can be His viceregent on the earth. Those two viewpoints gather together the two human natures—the slave and the viceregent, with one being the condition of the other.

Viceregency is the male, or active, principle toward the worlds, which are the perfect female, or receptive, principle toward God. "A human being has two transcriptions: an outward transcription and an inward transcription. The outward transcription corresponds to the macrocosm in its totality, while the inward transcription corresponds to the God."[45] That outward content of the human being corresponds to his enslavement, while the inward content proclaims lordship and viceregency.

The outward side reflects distance from God and His incomparability. The inward side mirrors closeness and man's nature in His image. The two of them reflect and bear witness to God's hands, which have made the human being.

The whole cosmos comes into existence through the marriage of the complementary divine names, the names of beauty and majesty. The first group of names is connected more closely to God's similarity, while the second group is connected to His incomparability. God's double relationship with created things results in the polar structure of humans: spiritual and corporeal, or formless and formal.[46]

Love is the impulse of oneness toward multiplicity, in order for it to be made manifest. But love is also the impulse of multiplicity, which is nothing other than duality, toward oneness. Here are both the cause and the aim of humanity: the satisfaction of the revelation of oneness has drawn this humanity, together with the world, into existence. The satisfaction of return will turn duality toward oneness.

That return takes place by rising up by the levels of the human core. The first is in the breast, at the level of the soul, which "leads to evil," where submission to the Higher, or Peace, occurs. The other is in the heart of the inspired soul, where the trust between the lower and the Higher is revealed. The third is in the inner core, where the "soul, which reproaches," dominates and where there is understanding of phenomena in Reality and with It. And the fourth is in the kernel, in the "soul in peace," where oneness is attained. That ascent is the removal of veils or clothing, one after the other, so that closeness and certainty shall be increased until duality is overcome.[47]

Why was man created? That is the key question and no single answer
to it is sufficient. But the tradition of the Hidden Treasure points to it:
"I was the Hidden Treasure," says the Creator, "so I loved to be
known. Hence I created the creatures." And man too was created. The
reason for that creation is, according to the divine pronouncement, the
Creator's wish to be known.

Through the totality of creation God made real His names, which
were all undivided in hiddenness. Through the creation every name acquired a phenomenon. Thus, the sign or phenomenon reveals that name
to openness, but at the same time keeps it there—in the Hidden Treasure. All the worlds disclose God and thus manifest His love. In them
all His names are revealed, divided, and scattered. Every phenomenon
or sign carries and represents one of His names. None embraces them
all, and is, therefore, also definable. Since the totality of existence is a
whole, which embraces all His names, and since no single phenomenon can do that, the worlds are indeterminable and inconstant. "No single one" here means nothing in the world apart from man.

All the names that are revealed, divided, and scattered in the worlds
are united and gathered together in man. He is the whole and therefore
both open and indeterminable. Encompassing all the names, he is
capable of the knowledge that God loves. Thus, the worlds are the
integral form, or transcription, of Divine oneness. And that is what
man is too. As such, he is what makes real God's love of knowledge.

But God is known only to Himself, and that is nothing other than the affirmation of His unknowability. And that makes man an inexhaustible secret. He is a whole, and thus outside the duality in which his existence is placed. To that should be immediately added that man as such is in the worlds. He belongs to them and they belong to him. He has reached here through descent or a series of marriages of the higher with the lower. In that descent it is possible to recognize five levels—superformal, then spiritual, presumptive, then sensible, and original. Those levels do not dominate one another. They are in full mutual openness and harmony. The characteristics of all the levels are gathered together in the marriage of the pure human being, freed from imbalance, with a wife who is pure location. Out of this is revealed the form of the pure human self.

The turning of the Real toward the form that attains existence surpasses all levels and all interventions. Thus that form acquires the brilliance of the Real in the perfect harmony of all levels. That brilliance is unlimited, pure and revealed in harmony with the properties, forms, and effects of all the levels. That is why the human form is the mirror of everything. "It is imbued with the characteristics of all the levels in such a way that all the properties of the levels are preserved without any change entering in upon the divine effusion and self-disclosure that emanates from this level of human perfection."[48]

When God says "I am!" His "I" remains speech to Himself, and thereby also hiddenness. Only with man's "I am" does the Divine "I" acquire manifestation as "I am to you," or "I and you," or "I and You." That separateness is such that it does not exclude the fullness of "I," and is therefore the proclamation of the Self through the self. Thus Jesus says to God: "You know what is in my mind, but I know not what is in Yours."[49]

The fact that the self does not know the Self means that it does not know itself either. And its realization lies in knowledge, or, what is the same, in the Self. And that is its love of itself in potential realization—unity with the Self. Its ignorance is revealed as the divergence between the visible and the invisible. Every state of the self is the relationship between these two. When duality disappears, the self is united in the testimony that "there is no self other than the Self." Then the self knows itself through the oneness that is revealed in multiplicity. The aspiration of the self to know itself is its love for unity with the Self.

The human self is divided into two contents that correspond to the heavens and the earth—the visible and the invisible, the spirit and the body. Human uprightness bears witness to the potential of the self to rise and descend along the vertical line linking the visible with the invisible and the spirit with the body. The raising up of the self or, what is the same, the lowering of the self means the power of the higher over the lower. The ultimate outcome of that is unity as the aim toward which love and knowledge lead. And the other way around: the lowering of the self or the distancing of the self is the strengthening of egoism or the neglect of oneness, which is confirmed by duality: "They know the outward show of this nether life, but of the life to come they are heedless."[50]

But the self as conditional is not potential without multiplicity. Every self is a place of revelation of the Self, and every other self is otherness ["you-ness," *Trans.*] with the same potential.[51] And what the self wants in otherness is the Self that is revealed in that duality as a third-person Other ["He-ness," *Trans.*]. As such this third Other encompasses all things through His Mercy and knowledge.[52] The fact that the self is drawn to otherness proclaims that the first sees through the second the affirmation of the conditionality of duality and the irresistible power of unity. Such an orientation by the self means limitless openness or comprehensiveness. It cannot be satisfied by anything other than fullness. The relationship of the self and the other is always the confirmation of borders or limits, while fullness is outside. That is why the self seeks in the other its liberation from every limit and, therefore, every division. It wants the third Other and nothing less than that.

THE MOST BEAUTIFUL EXAMPLE

To follow the Prophet means to love God. As fullness and being, God manifests Himself in His relationship toward emptiness and nonbeing. Thus, His love toward manifestation draws out into existence the duality that embraces the countless multiplicity of phenomena through which the fullness of God's Treasure is revealed. Everything that is in existence is imbued with that fullness and praises it. But, in order that this should be comprehensible, fullness takes emptiness as its wife or emptiness gives itself to fullness in marriage. Every moment is the child of that relationship. Everything in it springs from that duality and that marriage.

The testimony of fullness is the fact that the totality of existence praises it, that is the Praiser, who is manifested as the deepest nature of every person. That nature as complete revelation is testified by the Praiser—God's slave or God's Messenger. He is the revelation and confirmation of God's love. And in order to be what he is, his love of God is the testimony of the fullness that is in everything—in every sign on the horizon and in the self.

With his fullness of praise the Prophet makes manifest the possibility of human perfection, which is the revelation of Love, Goodness, and Truth. The Prophet is, thus, the witness of oneness as the inseparable Source and Confluence of all revelation. But he himself is the most complete humility in fulfilling his debt toward God. Those who follow him are not in debt to him, as may be seen in God's commandment "Say: 'For this I demand of you no recompense. I ask you only to love your kindred. He that does a good deed shall be repaid many times over.'"[53]

Thus, to love God and follow the Prophet means to love people as the potential of realizing their original nature, the Creator's Love of making Himself manifest in His creation.[54] Being close is shared human potential. It does not exclude anyone. That is the reason for stressing the debt toward the orphan and the stranger and for the commandment that evil be met with good,[55] because "it may well be that God will put good will between you and those with whom you have hitherto been at odds."[56] That is the essence, which Jesus expresses like this: "Thou shalt love the Lord thy God with all thy heart, and with all thy soul, and with all thy mind. This is the first and great commandment. And the second is like unto it, Thou shalt love thy neighbour as thyself. On these two commandments hang all the laws and the prophets."[57]

God is the Praised. But in His hiddenness He is both the Praised and the Praiser. In the inseparability of His hiddenness there is no praise like the relationship between the Praiser and the Praised. His will or love toward something is revealed as His Word: "When we decree a thing, We need only say: 'Be' and it is."[58] Thus, "We" is the essence that has desire or love as the reason for the creative word. Given that this essence is the Praiser, and the Praise, and the Praised, its divergence is equal—the essence as the Praised and the word as the Praiser, between which is Praise.

When all the levels of being are gathered together in the perfect man, then Praise is revealed in him as the word of the Praised, and then his return, or his desire, is to be the Praiser in whom the word as knowledge and being as the essence have attained unity. The Praiser is, therefore, a beacon, for he receives the light in the totality of descending from the invisible through separation in the worlds to human lowness. The Praiser is the most beautiful example, because he encompasses in himself all that is scattered in the worlds, so that there are no worlds as the unreal veil on the face of the Real. The Praiser's desire for the Praised is revealed as his most beautiful harmony.

The world in its totality is the Praiser, but that totality is gathered together in man. Man in his original nature is in perfect harmony with the world as Praiser. He is the image of the Merciful in a collected way, as the world is in its divided way.

The greatest human potential is voluntary realization through being the Praiser. When that is achieved, man's completeness is a person completely submissive to the Praised and dependent on Him. For only thus is the duality of the Real and the unreal, fullness and emptiness, revealed. Through man's will, he lives with reality and fullness. That is why he experiences the totality of being in the world and the self: there is nothing to which his self is not exposed and to which his answer is not faith in the Real. And when in his human nature he undergoes the greatest suffering, he is turned toward Mercy as his deepest and indestructible nature. When he experiences death, for him that is just the extreme that the duality of being as living, and nonbeing as dead, may reach without abandoning the fullness of oneness.

The Praiser is an orphan and terrified, depised and persecuted, wounded and poisoned, sick and bereaved, hungry and thirsty, denied and cursed. But out of all that is in existence, he turns to the nonexistent as the Origin, Source, and Confluence of the whole multiplicity. His love for phenomena passes over and above them, given that they are only signs of Him, face to face with whom the totality of the world is nothing.

Following

PRAISE

Praise is the relationship between the Praiser and the Praised. And
there is nothing in the horizons and the selves without it. The totality
of creation is its widespread revelation. Man gathers it together and it
is his uncreated core, so that there is no praise other than Praise. His
greatest potential is to be a Praiser in such a way that both he and the
horizons are revealed as Praise: "Then say: 'Praise be to God! He will
show you His signs, and you will recognize them.'"[1] Through this
recognition of Praise in the signs a man transforms his self toward
the perfection of the Praiser, who is "a good example,"[2] "a sublime
nature,"[3] "a shining light,"[4] "a blessing to mankind."[5]

Since Praise is always God's, all connection with Him is also receiving from the Praiser or "following him." And no one can meet
God, and that means neither can one attain Eternity without acknowledging the Praiser. Honor, glory, and Praise belong to the Praised.
Given that they are present in existence, and that they are revealed in
divergence in relation to their contradictory potential, they are the reality of phenomena. When they are present in discourse, they make
Him manifest, as Jesus says: "And I seek not mine own glory: there
is one that seeketh and judgeth. Verily, verily, I say unto you, If a
man keep my saying, he shall never see death."[6] "If I honour myself,"
continues Jesus, "my honour is nothing: it is my Father that honoureth
me; of whom ye say, that he is your God."[7] As may be concluded

from this, Praise belongs only to God and, as His revelation in every phenomenon, it is made inseparable from the question of the relationship between life and death.

He Who gives life is the Living. Death is, therefore, only a way of revealing the Living in creation or contingency. It is not a principle. Since Praise is revealed as the direct presence of the Praised in phenomena, it is not mediated, just as life is not either. And that direct presence of the Praised and the Living in space and time is revealed as Love, or unity with the Complete. Seeing life in a contingent way, in relation to death, demands the recognition that there is no living apart from the Living, nor self apart from the Self. Jesus says of this: "Therefore does my Father love me, because I lay down my life, that I might take it again. No man taketh it from me, but I lay it down of myself. I have power to lay it down, and I have power to take it again. This commandment have I received of my Father."[8]

The denial of life apart from Life is the condition for overcoming death. It is only through the return of all things to oneness and the recognition of it in the whole dispersal of creation that the Praiser recognizes the infinite closeness of the Praised in his love. "He that loveth life shall lose it; and he that hateth his life in this world shall keep it unto life eternal. If any man serve me, let him follow me."[9] To follow the one who is completely the Praiser, and therefore who loves God and whom He loves, means to be close to him and endeavor to identify with him. Thus, the follower of the Praiser loves him more than everything in existence, because that means to love God. And to love the Praiser and the Praised is to have their love. Those who testify that the Praiser is His slave and His emissary love one another, as Jesus also says: "That ye love one another, as I have loved you, that ye also love one another. By this shall all men know that ye are my disciples, if ye have love one to another."[10]

To love the Living, which means to testify that there is no living apart from Him, is to deny the contingent for the sake of the Complete. In order to live, says Jesus, one must fulfill the commandment "Thou shalt love the Lord thy God with all thy heart, with all thy soul, and with all they strength, and with all thy mind; and thy neighbour as thyself."[11] It is thus because testifying that there is no living apart from the Living means returning to oneness and unity with it or Love.

Thus, to give and to take and to love one's neighbor as oneself means to testify that there is no self other than the Self. When the self wishes to make itself manifest, it seeks to do so in the outer world. It is determined by the horizons with the countless multiplicity of signs within them. Opposite that outer world is the self, which wishes to be known, also in the countless multiplicity of signs within it. Establishing the mutuality of the outer and the inner, when the outer is scattered and distant, while the inner is collected and close, makes manifest oneness as its irreplaceable principle. The human core can gather the outer and the inner together only if it is outside the inclusiveness of the heavens and the earth, only if they are one of the possibilities in it.

Opposite the face is the Face. If the image wants the fullness of its origin, then it can be seen only through that Face. It confirms that I am Self. And there is nothing that could praise the self apart from that Self, which is the Praised. And as the image of the Praised, the self receives or reflects the properties of the Praised, thus becoming a witness of the Praiser as its model. And the Praiser is the most submissive, and as such is the most beautiful example in the manifestation of the Praised. Thus is loving in the self of the beloved the same as Praise in the self of the Praiser. They are the presence and manifestation of the Beloved and the Praised.

WITH THE PRAISER

The will turns away from phenomena in which Praise is not revealed, or it endeavors to discover it in them as veiled treasure. Praise found or revealed is the proclamation of Peace, and also the power of attraction. Thus the self opens up to the revelation of Praise where it is despised in forgetting God—in the poor and foreign, the weak and the dead. Steadfast following of the emissaries, who are always complete Praisers, is also a condition for opening up to God's love:

> Say: "If you love God, follow me.
> God will love you, and forgive you your sins.
> God is forgiving and merciful."[12]

God and the Praiser are in complete love. They love one another, and in the Praiser nothing is revealed apart from the Self, which knows Itself and knowledge of complete being. Here faith is the identity of love and knowledge: the beloved has become the known. "The most excellent faith is to love him who loves God, to hate him who hates God, to use the tongue ceaselessly in repeating the Name of God, to treat men as you would wish them to treat you and to reject for others what you would reject for yourselves."[13] Other than that love of God, which places a man on the path of following the Prophet, and thus including him in the love of everything that is in the horizons and selves as the possible follower of that ascent, there can be nothing else.

Every love of phenomena includes, directly or indirectly, following the Prophet. And that means to be the lover of God and His beloved. Through that opening up toward Praise for the sake of disclosing his essential conditionality, his exalted nature, and the most beautiful splendor, the human self withdraws before the Self as fullness and the oneness of being and knowledge: "The Prophet is nearer to the believers even than their selves."[14]

In this way man frees himself from the illusion in which the world is close and God distant, and draws closer to an understanding of the revealed as an image. In that image everything is from God and everything returns to Him. The world is thus indirect, and truth is not: it is the infinitely close and complete judgment of everything. God is a companion and other in everything, but no one and nothing is a companion and other to Him. The commonest illusion opposed to that is taking of parents as the cause of existence, children as a refuge, and society as the stage on which selves sufficient unto themselves are formed. That is the meaning of Jesus's interpretation: "If any man comes to me, and hate not his father, and mother and wife, and children, and brethren, and sisters, yea, and his own life also, he cannot be my disciple."[15] That "hating" those whom he otherwise loves, including also his own self, means nothing other than the testimony that there is no self other than the Self. For the Real is the Self. It is the truth and one. Man is made real in so far as he is open to Completeness or in so far as the unreality in him is denied, as Jesus says: "If any man will come after me, let him deny himself, and take up his cross and follow me."[16]

Thus, every connection with another becomes transformed through that love of God, which, by following the Praiser, is transformed into God's love of the follower, for whom God and His Prophet are dearer than the father, the child, and all people.[17] Although a person is in a constant relationship with the outer world, all his details and he as a whole are what is not God.

But there is nothing in the horizons or in the selves that is not submissive to Him. In the Completeness of that submission every phenomenon in existence and existence as a whole make God manifest. He is, thus, incomparable and distant, but also similar and close. He reveals Himself in the totality of creation, remaining always and everywhere present otherness. Everything in existence is the disclosure of His Self. And that as disclosure praises Him Who is hidden.

The cause of the disclosure is love for it. That is why Praise is the repayment of that love. The Praiser in his fullness is sent with words which include everything,[18] or, as he says, "I came to know everything in the heavens and the earth."[19] Coming to know everything that is in existence is the same as the disclosure of the Praised to the Praiser in which Praise and knowledge are one and the same.

The Praiser is, thus, the "place" in which love is revealed as knowledge, and the other way around. The Praiser accepts Praise in his complete submission and it transforms him into the one to whom the signs in the horizons and selves are submissive: they become the same as his self, they disclose the love of the hidden for manifestation.

HATRED AND FEAR

"Those who hate God" are none other than individuals who have taken the signs in the horizons and selves, denied what they are and given them names and meaning beyond their Origin and Purpose. They have adopted phenomena from the horizons and selves as causes and consequences, and they attribute creative properties to them. Thus nonbeing and evil have become a beginning out of which the measurable world is drawn and presented as the only possible one. The feeling that phenomena, projects, and structures are independent is transformed into closedness of both the horizons and the selves. That is choosing a god other than God, and reducing Praise to the closedness of the world and the contingent self as its builder and director, which is nothing other than hatred of Him.

From such a perspective, signs are not windows from one level of existence onto another. Through them it is not possible to pass by and beyond the heavens. Arrogance and denial darken them, and they become gods that inhabit the world around the human core, transforming it into closedness and rigidness. No way out of that closedness is possible without the hatred of "those who hate God," through which they too, in their original potential, include also followers of the Prophet, whereby their hatred is seen as the stiffening of the self to the point of petrification and sickness.

Thinking that sacrifices itself in speech here meets what is for it an insoluble riddle: to hate one's parents[20] and to love one's enemies,[21] and to respond to evil with good,[22] to love one's neighbor as oneself,[23] and the Praiser more than oneself,[24] one's children, parents, and all people. The riddle is insoluble as long as all phenomena and changes in the world are separated from true Reality; as long as a man wants anything less than being and the self as the one and only Completeness; as long as he associates anything with God. And this insolubility means that beauty and love are only illusions and that they are, in essence, hatred, for they transpose fear of God onto fear of phenomena in the horizons and the selves. The cause becomes what gives birth, and the aim, what is born.

From such an illusory perspective, liberation is offered as power over the horizons and the selves, and not as the inclusion of the will in Peace as the source and Confluence of all things. The idea of complete fatherhood and "sonhood" fills the closed selves and their world. Since association with God has become the predominant custom, and that means taking nonbeing as the Creator, beauty and goodness are only names for ugliness and evil. In the Teaching it is said of that relationship, "Think! Who, beside God, can guide the man who makes his lust his god?"[25] and "Yet there are some who worship idols, bestowing on them the adoration due to God."[26]

The other side of this is Jesus's invitation to hatred of one's parents as the illusion of the immediate cause of existence, which is expressed in another way in the Teaching: "Say: 'Come, I will tell you what your Lord has made binding on you: that you shall serve no other gods beside Him; that you will show kindness to your parents; that you shall not kill your children because you cannot support them.'"[27] The mention of the killing of children, which is only one of the more explicit statements about general killing, points to the raising up of the contingent self to the level of a god, who gives both life and death. Fear of poverty is nothing other than ignorance about being and the self, the consequence of which is adopting dependence on the world rather than on God. Thus, adopting the world and ruling it is experienced as wealth, and that stimulates and feeds greed: "Your hearts are taken up with worldly gain from the cradle to the grave. But you shall learn. Then you shall surely learn."[28]

Fear of the world and concern for its adopted part increasingly transform a man, for they distance him from Peace and weaken his will to resist it through a great war in the self.[29] His self becomes increasingly stiff and rigid. The outer world appears incomplete and unfinished, so its transformation is undertaken, which, in the end, is shown as sullying, devastation, and killing. Opposed to this stands God's command: "Have no fear of them; fear Me."[30]

That command is nothing other than the invitation to turn to Mercy, which encompasses everything, for God says: "My mercy encompasses all things."[31] For how could man's essential neediness be confirmed—"God does not need you, but you need Him!"[32]—without fear of Completeness? Without such fear and that neediness a man could not be open to God's complete Mercy. And the stiffness and rigidity of the self that sees itself as Completeness would move toward disintegration or nothingness, which is not possible since, in itself, nothingness cannot confirm existence.

Fear of God is the confirmation that existence is and is not God, and that human freedom of choice, which springs from trust offered and accepted, is always also involvement in that "is not" or that "nothingness."[33] Man's distance from God is revealed as his forgetfulness of God and turning toward nothingness, which manifests itself as the evil of createdness, darkness that thickens, conjuring witches, and the mischief of the envier when he envies.[34]

Through his fear man confirms what he is and what he can be by returning to God: man fears God, but He does not fear him. God judges man, but man does not judge Him. To fear God means to recognize punishment for sin and the torment of shame, the relationship of consequences and causes in existence, and that means also in action. To love God means to bear witness to Him by accepting what brings one closer to Him and turning away from everything that takes one further from Him.

UNITY

The expectation of mercy, hope in Mercy, and leading toward Mercy through the statement "in the Name of God the Compassionate, the Merciful" transforms the heart from roughness to full tenderness, when it becomes like that of a bird.[35] And the devil, which means unreality and nothingness, threatens a man with poverty,[36] while the transformation of the self into independence and sufficiency leads him from the position of keeper of the created world into competition with the Creator. By accepting poverty, along with fear of God, the human self opens toward the Wealthy One and passes through the degrees of "melting of the heart," in order to receive into itself the Praiser. This is the persistence of the will, which, by saying "no," wages war against illusions in the horizons and the selves.

The contingent self inclines toward the Self and existence toward Being. In that ascent a man wants nothing other than God. The worlds are not sufficient for him. Thus the Self in knowledge overcomes the self:

And the most beloved things with which My slave comes nearer to Me is what I have enjoined upon him; and My slave keeps on coming closer to Me through supererogatory works until I love him, so I become his hearing with which he hears, and his sight with which he sees, and his hand with which he grips, and his

leg with which he walks; and if he asks Me, I will give him, and
if he asks my protection, I will protect him.[37]

Given that everything disappears apart from God's Face and that it is
before a man wherever he may turn, the face of a woman makes manifest the relationship of the Praiser and the Praised. The beauty that
that beauty makes manifest bears witness to the way of love as drawing close to Him Who remains behind the veil although He is made
manifest in all things. "Three things of this world of yours made it
lovable to me," says the Praiser, "women, perfume and prayer—in
which lies the coolness of my eye."[38] This famous statement contains
the totality of the holy tradition. The speaker is the Praiser and he is
addressing all mankind. He calls the world in which he is speaking
"this world of yours." This directly indicates that this world is more
theirs than his, given that his essence is Praise of God and full liberty
made real in perfect enslavement to Him. Thus, love, which is the
principle of existence, is disclosed in him: God loves him and he loves
God. He is the highest potential of man as such. Given that this world
is drawn out as the shadow or image of the other, which is immeasur-
ably more real and therefore also better, that higher world belongs to
the Praiser. His speech to mankind makes him manifest for them as
the most beautiful example in that only God is Reality, which the
worlds make manifest. In order to show that "this world" is only the
starting point toward Reality, the Praiser distinguishes its three signs.

Opposed to man himelf, in the conditions following his fall, in
which, nevertheless, his original most beautiful uprightness was not
lost, is woman as the manifestation of man to himself. What man sees
in woman is himself. The totality of his existence recognizes his Creator in that image. But, that image is known only to his heart, which
God turns as he wishes between His two fingers, as the unrepeatable
phenomenon of every instant. Beauty or the fullness of eternity is
made manifest in the figure of woman. The figure and what it manifests are reconciled in outwardness and inwardness, but, despite the
attraction of what that figure proclaims, it remains limited.

Everything that is limited vanishes, while God's Face is always and everywhere. That duality of the figure and eternity is transformed into a scent—beauty without an image. Thus is limitation overcome. A connection is established with the border of phenomena. That by means of which one sees and what is seen become united.

And prayer is the connection of the outward and inward.[39] In the fullness of this connection the Praised sees with the Praiser's eye.

The turning of the heart, which is between God's two fingers, transforms the totality of the world's outwardness into the whole of human inwardness. The countless multiplicity of marriages as a way of the world's existing in that turning of the heart is carried over into the marrying nature of the self. Every sign in the horizon has two sides—the visible and the invisible. The invisible is closer to the origin than the visible. The invisible marries the visible. That marriage in which the visible marries the invisible makes actual the universal interaction of the two in the testimony and constant revelation of oneness.

The totality of existence is in that giving and taking in marriage that is expressible as God's creation of the First Intelligence, or the Pen. That First Intelligence is completely subject to the Creator. On the other hand, the "first material," or the Tablet, is entirely subject to the First Intelligence. The totality of existence gives itself in marriage to that inscription of the Pen on the Tablet. That succession of marriages in the outer world corresponds to the succession within each human being—spirit, soul, and body. The interdependence between God and the world is expressed in human interdependence. Giving and taking in marriage in each case are fitting names for that interdependence and interconnectedness. The sexual relation of the male and the female is the decisive sign of duality as witness and manifestation of oneness.

THE LOVE OF A WOMAN

By seeing beauty in the figure of woman, man discloses himself. That is his relaxation or sobriety before the possibility of disclosing himself in the outer world. What is disclosed is revealed as separateness from himself. In it he sees a sign about God. Out of sobriety before this revelation he passes into drunkenness: he loves God, but what is revealed to him flees and vanishes. Wherever the drunken man turns, there he finds a trace of the Beloved. But that trace does not endure even for one moment, nor does it accept the lover's reaching for him in any form. He is everywhere and nowhere, so the lover is in a state of constant wandering and collision.

He loves God, but he does not find requital for his love. Does God love me? he asks. The interrelationship between the Praiser and the Praised is disclosed in him as the latter speaking in the former: "If you love God, follow me, and God will love you." To follow the Praiser means to get to know oneself, in order for it to be made apparent that there is no self other than the Self. With that and from that springs God's Love toward what is laid bare before God, accepting the Praiser as its best example.

The order of loving God and following the Praiser is established here as a condition of God's Love for man. But what is conditional here is essentially different: God's Love for man is unconditional and primary, since He created man in love so as to manifest Himself.

God's Love is eternal and timely: "He is with you, wherever you are."[40]

God has always been and will always be One and the same. All phenomena, both as undivided in His secret and as divided in His creation, are not and cannot be anything other than His unchangeable being. God praises the Praiser, while he loves Him.

Of what is in this world, women have been made lovable to the Praiser. Humanity is the presence of the spirit and soul. Perfect humanity is the harmony of the spirit as the male and active principle and the soul as female and receptive. That harmony proclaims oneness, as the everywhere and always present Face. To know the soul or the self means to know the Lord. The need for that is love, and that is love of God. To love a woman means to love God. And here is the greatest secret of love. There is no greater satisfaction than the greatest closeness with a woman and unity with her. But, that satisfaction is nothing other than the revelation of God. If the participants in it attribute it to anything other than closeness to God, that amounts to fixation with place and moment of revelation and ignoring Him Who reveals Himself then and there. After every such satisfaction thorough cleansing is demanded, so that the participants in that union should deny that any such fixation may be attributed to them.

Neither the place nor the time of the revelation of goodness and beauty may be replaced by what is revealed. Unity and satisfaction in unity can be known only through return to multiplicity and contingency. Pureness is the refusing to accept multiplicity for anything other than the oneness that is proclaimed in it. Love transforms hiddenness into knowledge. That is how oneness is revealed in multiplicity. And when it is revealed, multiplicity is that same oneness. The act of cleansing after union confirms that oneness in multiplicity and multiplicity in oneness.

Every attribution of satisfaction in that momentary revelation stimulates the jealousy and wrath of Him Who discloses Himself. And that is bowing down to and servitude to the selves other than the Self, contrary to His revelation in the Torah: "Thou shalt not bow down thyself to them, nor serve them: for I the Lord thy God am a jealous God."[41]

Sobering from intoxication and confusion means understanding that all the horizons, both the heavens and the earth, have been created and dispersed only so that they should be gathered together in man. All that is in the horizons, both the heavens and the earth, does not encompass Him Who is the aim of human knowledge. That is why man's love, as a force that leads him on the path of understanding, is arranged for passing through the worlds and past them, as far as Him Who has made His oneness manifest in that greatness of the heavens and the earth and in the human heart, which encompasses all things. Everything in existence is subordinate to man with the condition that his essence is Praise of God.

God does not abandon man even when he is in deepest forgetfulness. Man's remembrance is the disclosure in himself of unforgetting as a principle, which is God's love of making Himself manifest. The disclosure of that principle of creation means the testimony that there is no self other than the Self. "And whosoever knows himself, knows his Lord," says the Praiser. He loves them, and they love Him is the principle of love that enables man to disclose and surrender to himself.[42] By doing so through following the Praiser the lover draws close to God.

And drawing close is the disclosure of perfection as the highest human potential. That perfection is in submission. Every good begins in openness to its acceptance. And that is a relationship of speech and listening. The one who speaks takes into account a listener who is silent. And he would like the one who is silent to hear and understand him in full beauty. The speaker expects of the listener complete openness for receiving what is heard. In speech is revealed activeness, or maleness, but it is observed from the "place" of reception, or femaleness. Thus, the satisfaction of action is achieved in the acquiescence of the receiver, or in the "self at peace."

In the sexual act the self is overcome by the strength of satisfaction, which gives a premonition of the bliss of heavenly proximity to

God. That satisfaction makes manifest God's severity toward His tenderness. The mutuality of severity and tenderness corresponds to greatness and beauty, wrath and mercy. Submission to severity, power, and wrath, in that orientation toward unity, does not lead to distancing, but to incomparable satisfaction.

In woman a man reveals his self and wishes to see it without clothes or veil and to clear away his duality:

> If the soul were stripped of all her sheaths, God would be discovered all naked to her view and would give himself to her, withholding nothing. As long as the soul has not thrown off all her veils, however thin, she is unable to see God.[43]

The separation of the earth and heavens, as a duality that confirms oneness, has its resolution in man, for whom it is a home in his highest potential. He returns to that home like a traveler. He establishes contact with it and does so through woman, who reveals herself in everything on that path, as the Praiser says:

> A forenoon journey or an afternoon journey in Allah's Cause is better than the whole world and whatever is in it; and a place equal to an arrow bow of any one of you, or a place equal to a foot in Paradise is better than the whole world and whatever is in it; and if one of the women of Paradise looked at the earth, she would fill the whole space between them (the earth and the heaven) with light, and would fill whatever is in between them with perfume, and the veil of her face is better than the whole world and whatever is in it.[44]

Undressing and Union

What is lowered down must also be raised up. Descent includes also ascent. So it is also with separation and unification. At the beginning of separation its participants are closest. Their forms do not entirely cover up the oneness of their essence. By moving away from that essence, the form becomes more closed and more opaque. While the child grows in its mother's womb, for all that it is acquiring specificity, it remains part of her. The unity of the child and the mother in the womb bears witness to the Mercy of oneness: the unborn child is subordinate to that world of inner Mercy, and is a viceregent in it. The transformation of the full unity of mother and child into their specificity and separation is revealed as love.

Remembrance of unity and the experience of parting impose the need for a name through which the growing distance should be bridged. He who can be bodily absent and distant remains close in the memory and the name. Children are born naked. Their nakedness is prolonged as a reminder of original oneness. But the distance becomes ever greater and seeing from that distance reveals that unity has been lost, and that it is possible to attain it by acknowledging the reality of separateness and specificity. And that is clothing.

Man and woman hide their nakedness. Clothes confirm separateness, but also the return to oneness. As long as the world is a veil in which everything is acknowledged as a sign, man does not know his nakedness. But as soon as that transparency disappeared in the first man, the acknowledgement of the world as createdness began to demand clothing and a turning to inwardness as one and outwardness as the other side of the self. By increasing the distance and forgetfulness of original unity, clothing and veiling become decisive forms of the revelation of reality.

The love between parents and children, brothers and sisters, and other relatives springs from a feeling of closeness in the oneness from which they grow distant. Love for people as such bears witness to the feeling of necessary oneness at some beginning. But all those feelings, which are always in a greater or lesser degree of forgetfulness, remain behind human orientation in time. Such orientation is always within borders, which are indicated by clothing and veils.

The oneness that is at the beginning is not lost forever. It is the potential of every person, since it was once complete. That is why separation is at the same time also the possibility of unclothing in fullness before it. Unification is the necessity of separation and the other way around. And that unification is turned toward fullness and closeness. It is revealed in drawing near to the veils and passing behind them. Multiplicity is only the revelation of oneness. The relationship between all participants in that multiplicity is one of connection with oneness.

All forms of friendship are the realization and confirmation of the common and the close. The strength with which one endeavors to overcome and surpass separation is love. And the source of love is that oneness. The fact that man, like everything else, is created in Reality and with It, that It is with him wherever he is, that It is closer to him than his jugular vein, that It is everywhere he turns, that It responds to him when he calls, that It remembers him when he remembers It—all this enables him to return constantly from multiplicity to oneness and to do so by innumerable paths.

The first man was really close to God, and he was naked. The forbidden tree and his heart were not separated. What was forbidden in the outer world was forbidden in his core. Through the pureness in

those two cores, which were, in fact, one and the same core, the totality of the Garden was also in a state of complete pureness. When man
opposed his will to God's, the prohibition in his inwardness was revealed as separate from the prohibition in the outer world. By trans-
gressing the prohibition he lost his original closeness to the Creator,
which existed alongside his clear consciousness that he was merely a
creature.

Up until that loss he had seen the Face in everything—equally in
its concentration in the face of woman and in the totality of existence.
That transgression "separated" him from the fullness of Mercy and
the Face became veiled, so his gaze tried uneasily to pass through the
signs, which suddenly became impenetrable. Before the transgression
of the prohibition the phenomena in the Garden were transparent.
They all manifested the truth with which they were created. The nakedness of his wife was just as transparent, and she had nothing other
than the beauty through which the Creator revealed Himself. Satan
whispered to them words against the prohibition, in order, by trans-
gressing it, to make their bodies impenetrable, so that their nakedness
would be revealed to them, and thus also borders and separateness.

And when they saw themselves in this way, they reached for the
leaf of paradise in order to cover their nakedness and ensure that the
inwardness of both their specificities should be preserved for the new
unity for which they hoped.[45] But unity presupposes undressing and
union. It confirms that it is they, rather than anything else in the world,
who make manifest all God's names. The human being is fullness,
and everything else is a part. The human being is in the center of existence, and everything else is on the edge. The undressing and uniting
of husband and wife is the confirmation of oneness as the beginning
and the end. In that process two principles are revealed—the active
and the receptive, the male and the female, as the flowing oneness
where everything in existence is, but always also as separation, which
seeks and confirms oneness.

Separateness and distance aim, in different ways, toward closeness
and unity. A person can disclose himself to another person. But his

disclosure to another person is at the same time also concealment. Through that concealment in disclosure or through that dressing in undressing she and he become for one another as clothing. They exclude the gaze of the world and turn toward one another for the sake of revealing the heavenly state of pureness and closeness. Through the touching of their bodies they transform speech into being.

The inconstancy of listening, speaking, and watching is transformed into the inconstancy of touch. They endeavor to "put together" the borders of their selves and to unite their essences behind the form. The greater the drawing closer, the shorter time it lasts. The height of their union is momentary and transient. After that, oneness is revealed again in a clear sense of separateness with increased sorrow and weariness. The constant Flow is revealed through both separateness and touching, but it remains the inexorable oneness, which both rejects and accepts everything that it is not. Thus, opposed to its eternity is time filled with the surging sound of reality. That surge of time both testifies to and denies mercy. It is extinguished when unity is achieved. And nothing other than unity overcomes separation.

Knowledge

THE STATION OF NO-STATION

The deeper and more wide-ranging one's reflections about love are, the clearer it becomes that it is not definable. The directedness that is felt and sought in love is revealed in the very impossibility of defining it through nondirectedness. Although the will is the starting point of every reflection about love, it leads only to the borders, so that it should be testified there that they, those limits of the definable, confirm the nonexisting as fullness.

The will sets out from the illusion that forms the human standpoint and endeavors to transform it into something higher and different. But that transformation is an ascent to standlessness, or the openness of the heart to fullness and uprightness. In the laying down of any kind of standpoint the will endeavors to transform itself into love. And that means that the will turns out of the world and away from it toward uprightness or the origin of creation, but that never happens without a secret interconnection with knowledge.

The question of the relationship of knowledge and love is decisive for both of them. If it is possible to say that the will turns man away from his self toward the Divine Self, or from existence toward nonexistence, and that, thus, love is "rooted" in the will, the opposite is felt to be the case with knowledge: what is known to man is what has come from the Intellect to become understanding, skill, and the art of creation.

In the state of love man is poor and a beggar in front of the person he loves. The person in love endeavors to see, feel and know himself through the beloved. He adapts his self in order that, in his being identified with the beloved, it should look beautiful to him. The person in love seeks in his self the manifestation of beauty for the beloved. That manifestation, toward the feeling and aspiration of the one in love, would make his self attractive to the beloved. Thus, the attributes of the beloved—speech, listening, looking, and so forth—are nothing other than the attributes of the one in love. But, since all these attributes are forever veiled and since behind them lies the essence of oneness and the oneness of essence, the one in love knows that nothing can be achieved other than the possibility of impossibility: that ear through which the one in love hears himself through the beloved, just like all his other potential, is one and the same ear through which oneness listens to itself.

That is why the one in love is a beggar to himself. All his endeavors to find his beloved in the greatness and beauty of the outer world return him, confused and weary, to him himself. His self offers and reveals itself as a veil on the face of the loved one. His seeking, calling, and knocking are turned toward that side, toward the darkness of the self. In that darkness he wishes to find the path to the house and threshold of his beloved. When he has reached that threshold, he calls and knocks, expecting her to respond from the other side and that she will open the door to him. He is prepared to reveal himself to her and give himself to her completely naked, alone with half of his debt of oneness, to offer himself to her as a robe to wrap around her. He expects her to reveal herself and give herself to him completely naked, like his missing half. The commandment to say "Our God and your God is One"[1] is transformed in him into "My God and thy God is One." And God says: "I am God; there is no god but Me."[2] Thus, the "I" that calls and knocks seeks and expects to see himself in the "you" who responds. That self of the caller and the self of the one who responds are a duality in which the totality of existence is revealed. They know one another and join in oneness as a third-person self. The self as I offers itself to the self as you as its clothing, for it has nothing other than itself. And the self as you has nothing other than the self as I, and so it too offers itself as clothing. That turning of the self as I to the self as you testifies to the third-person self as oneness. Their separation makes every instant a new creation, but always out of oneness and toward it.

All that the one in love has is only a veil in front of the beloved. And he wishes that the beloved reveal herself to him without clothing—she to him, just as he to her. In that revelation, they feel, the intermediary of speech that passes by means of the voice through the hidden would disappear: their skins would speak as the borders that touch and join. What would speak would be the instant in which their duality is joined in one and the same unfolding in which their totality is surrendered to the unknownness of the seed—to the seventh day or the seventh ray.

In knowledge, man looks through phenomena and reads them as sayings about the one he loves. And since God is beautiful and since He loves beauty, He reveals Himself as beauty to the one who knows the world. Loving what is revealed is complete poverty before what is beautiful: since God is beautiful, he loves Himself. Both beauty and love are His manifestation to Himself. But, His love of being known demands otherness, and it can be none but Him. Thus, God manifests Himself to Himself through creation and all its potential—from the lowest detail, to its totality.

Therefore, the face of man is opposite the Face of God. And God is oneness. He sees Himself in that human face and therefore descends to full closeness. He is before him in everything, but never completely disclosed to anyone other than Himself, for His closeness is complete. She is the oneness of which all other proximities are only signs. And in order for that closeness to be complete in the human self, the totality of existence or the manifestation of oneness requires "returning" from dispersal or separation into enduring oneness.

The place of that return is the heart. Seen from the world, it is "infinitely tiny." But in it love has achieved complete unity, and knowledge is transformed into complete being. Given that the totality of creation is in it and with it, the heart is open to the countless multiplicity of existence, but nevertheless, is both with it and outside it. All phenomena in the heart are undivided potential—both confirmed and united. Neither constancy nor closedness are possible for its openness. Its oneness that gives itself in everything and takes from everything gathers together both the Creator and the creature in oneness. No station is outside it, but the heart is not reducible to any one of them. Its openness is the station of no-station.

Given that every phenomenon has an innumerable multitude of outer and inner aspects in its coming from oneness and returning to it, only the heart is ready to ensure for it a path in which the lower surrenders to the higher, and so on into infinity, into a limitless multitude of giving and taking in marriage. In it every phenomenon turns constantly, so as itself to see itself in the fullness of its discourse about the Hidden Who loves to be known.

THE SPEECH OF SKINS

Whenever anyone praised the Imam 'Ali, he would respond that he knew himself better than others did, but that God knew him better than any.[3] As this statement says, a man can hide from another man, and even from himself, but he cannot hide from God. Since the eyes, ears, and skin are the borders across which relationships are established between the self and the nonself, they are also obstacles for the other in his knowledge of the inner self. Thus hearing, sight, and touch bear witness to what can be hidden from another. And only those who can speak can bear witness.

Human reliance on the other's lack of knowledge about his inner self presupposes the inability of ears, eyes, and skin to speak. They are thus subordinated to human management through speech. This removes from them their nature as signs that return to the designated objects, handing on to them all that it has accepted from them. What is hidden in human closedness, through ears, eyes, and skin, cannot be unknown to their Creator. Hiding from another in the outer world transforms man into a god if it is denied that nothing was ever hidden from God.

The uncovering of the body, the openness of the eyes, and hearing render a man naked in front of the other. But he can also cover himself before the other. Closing his eyes or turning his gaze away, not listening or blocking his ears. But, none of this makes him hidden from God. Everything of his remains accessible to Him.

Forewarn them of the day when the enemies of God will be
brought together and led into the Fire, so that when they enter it,
their ears, their eyes and their very skins will testify
to their misdeeds: "Why did you speak against us?"
they will say to their skins, and their skins will reply:
"God, who gives speech to all things, has made us speak.
It was He who in the beginning created you, and to Him
shall you be recalled. You did not hide yourselves,
so that your ears and eyes and skins could not be made
to testify against you. Yet you thought that God
did not know much of what you did.
It was the thoughts you entertained about your Lord
that ruined you, so that you are now among the lost."[4]

Man's presence in the world, through touch and exchange, includes
the skin as a border. But human totality is contact with the outer world
across open and closed borders. Man is never completely open, nor
completely closed to the outer world. And this indicates his place on
the border between this world and the higher one. If he is closed
toward the higher, the outward penetrates into his inner self as into a
yawning pit. But if it is open to the higher world, his inner self is also
illuminated by light, which is elementally higher than that in the outer
world. Then the outer world is illuminated through it.

God is the complete Witness. And everything that reaches into the
inner world from the outer one, across the open and closed borders of
the self, bears witness to those borders. Only thought can deny that,
but together with closure toward the Higher. Then man is reduced to
separation from the Real. By raising his thinking to the highest level,
he adjudges to himself separation from the Real. The consequence of
this is the impossibility of any relationship between evil and good.
They become two opposed principles that are in insoluble struggle.
Only in the openness of the self toward the principle can that insoluble
duality take on a completely different aspect:

Good deeds and evil deeds are not equal.
Requite evil with good.[5]

Being in the skin, or borders, means the separation of the self and the world. That separation reflects another: all that is divergent in the world as a whole is gathered together in man. His center, or heart, "stands" on the border between the spirit and the body. Through it the light of the spirit is carried into the world of the soul. When human divergence is directed toward oneness as its aim, only that center can anticipate every change. It does not permit any form to have permanence, for that can be nothing other than a sign of oneness. That is why unity is the removal of clothing and veils, the opening of naked skins to one another, so that separation should be touched and denied. Touching and kissing are like the transition from one side of existence to the other, so that the self should be closer to the Self. But the Self is only present in the pure heart. Touching and kissing and union at the moment of achieving the peak of satisfaction, which unites severity and beauty and extinguishes separation, serve only to show that all dividedness and all closeness are different ways of disclosing that oneness.

And when the speech of divided speakers and listeners is transformed into the speech of skins, drawing near and unity are reflected in increasing serenity: "Their skins and their hearts melt at the remembrance of God."[6] "The remembrance of God" is in the center, or heart, of the human being. Every detail in existence has its double from which it is divided. That state of duality is the revelation of oneness, which is made manifest in His love. The skin is a veil that is necessary to knowledge, but love does not want any border with the Face of the Beloved. It cannot be satisfied by anything other than unity.

"God's veil is light," says the Prophet. "Were He to remove it, the glories of His face would burn away everything perceived by the sight of his creatures."[7] Love does not want anything other than that "burning away" of the self in the Self. For it no satisfaction other than that is acceptable. Remembrance of oneness, just like orgasm, confirms divergence as the revelation of Reality and unity as return to It.[8] The satisfaction of "touching oneness" in orgasm is not and cannot be transformed into Reality itself. It is accessible only in the complete burning away of the self. And that is the meaning of compulsory washing after orgasmic union: the skins testify to the oneness in multiplicity and multiplicity in oneness.

The mature separation of the male and the female testifies to oneness as their complete otherness in the act of undressing, caressing, kissing, and orgasm. All that is the path toward primary oneness. After that union of the male and the female and the momentary transformation of their duality into oneness there occurs the return to duality. And that return demands the repeated confirmation of water as the sign of creation, or the presence of oneness in every multiplicity. In crossing the border of the skin, in touching, kissing, and orgasm what occurs is that return to water out of which all of life has come[9] and to the drop out of which man is made.[10]

Both water and the drop conceal the possibilities that are revealed in human maturity. Kissing and orgasm unite the mature revelation of them as the first and last things, their outwardness and inwardness. Thus creation or the manifestation of oneness is connected with the hiddenness out of which everything comes and to which everything returns. To love means to kill oneself for the sake of life in another, and that is another whom no one resembles and who has no companion, that other who is as such infinitely close to everything. The life of everything is accepted as a gift from the Living and it is to Him that it returns.

THE SELF AND THE SELF

The well-known holy saying, in which God speaks through the Praiser, gathers together the relationship of knowledge and love: "I was the Hidden Treasure, so I loved to be known. Hence I created the creatures." The words "I was the Hidden Treasure" mean that the fullness of knowledge is in nonexistence or noncreatedness. It is there and thus eternally and forever. God's "I am" is the eternal fullness of knowledge. In that eternal and unchangeable fullness of knowledge, in which nothing is divided, lies love of knowledge. Therefore, the hiddenness of the treasure is God's love of knowledge. That love of knowledge has two contents—descending, from the Intellect toward man and ascending, from man toward the Intellect.

The first content is the Intellect through which the image of the Hidden Treasure is carried over into existence as a whole. The Intellect is, as the first appearance of creation, darkness in relation to the fullness of uncreated light. But it is light in relation to the soul that is illuminated by it. And the soul is darkness in relation to the Intellect although it is itself light in relation to the body. In that succession Intellect-soul-body the receptive level is transformed into the active. The Intellect receives everything from the Creator, but it acts on the soul.

"The Universal Soul arises from the First Intellect," says Ibn al-'Arabi. "Hence it is the first object of activity to arise from a created thing. It mixes that which acts upon it, with that upon which it acts. That which acts upon it is light, while that upon which it acts is darkness, that is, Nature."[11]

Everything that is in the Hidden Treasure will be revealed in the world and in man—dispersed through the world, and gathered together in man. That totality of revelation is one and the same man—the perfect image of God. God knows him and he knows God. In relation to one another, they are God's looking at Himself. Thus, creation emerges from Love, which is eternal. Given that in nonexistence there is no change, neither is the Love of God for Himself any different.

> The love God has for His creatures is without beginning or end.
> . . . He has never stopped loving His creatures just as He has never stopped knowing them. . . . His existence has no beginning, therefore His love has no beginning![12]

If one starts from the divergence of "love" and "knowledge," it is possible to say that the loving and attracting nature, whose standpoint is based on the duality of "generosity" versus "egoism," one comes upon the danger of neglecting the "objective truth." But the nature of the intellect, which, on the contrary, sees phenomena in the concepts "truth" versus "error," is exposed to the danger of neglecting purely human perfection, and even perhaps also the human connection with God. Although neither love nor knowledge appears in its pure form, it is possible to determine and distinguish them in different ways: "For the 'volitional' or 'affective' man, (the *bhakta*)," says Frithjof Schuon, "God is 'He' and the ego is 'I,' whereas for the 'Gnostic' or 'intellective' man (the *jnani*) God is 'I'—or 'Self'—and the ego is 'he' or 'other.'"[13] Here one should immediately observe that the revelation is expressible only in the mutual relation of the self and the Self. Given that it is brought down into the language of the self, as the discourse of the Self, it is brought down, spoken and given by Him, and heard, accepted, and repeated by the self. Thus, when that self says, "In the Name of God the Compassionate, the Merciful: praise be to God, Lord of the Universe or Our Father Who art in heaven," in those formulations, He and Thee are opposed to the self, but so is the self itself. The question of whose speech is expressed demands the resolution of the duality of the self and the Self. Consequently, the relation of the selves in the pattern "there is no—other than" can be revealed in two ways.

The first relation is the connection of the self to the Other. It reveals the perfection outside itself as the undeniable presence of beauty and goodness in the totality of revelation. The fact that beauty and goodness are present in everything that is outside the self obliges one to a debt toward them. Generosity and submissiveness are the connection with them. That is giving, which cleanses from the self the presence of the unreal. It is through giving that the self opens toward the Self.

The other way the relation may be revealed is the acceptance that perfection resides in the self, and that it must be disclosed. What reaches it from outside increases its hiddenness, so it shrinks from the world as revelation of otherness. Such shrinking, which is the opposite of the attractiveness in the first way, is revealed as sobriety, reasonableness, and the dominance of emotions.

The repeated question about the division of the self from the Self and the possibility of overcoming that duality is connected also with the saying about the two seas: "It was He who sent the two seas rolling, the one sweet and fresh, the other salt and bitter, and set a rampart between them, an insurmountable barrier."[14] The sweet sea corresponds to the spirit, and the salt one to the body. The barrier between them is the presumed world or the joining of the higher and the lower or the light and dark in one and the same revelation. If the higher world is light, it is fullness; if the lower world is darkness, it is nothingness. The visible world is light in relation to darkness or nothingness, but it is dark in relation to the invisible world.

The overcoming of that separateness is possible only in the full light that annihilates every division, and thus also every revelation. The world is, therefore, a revelation that is not possible without darkness. It is not God, and therefore a duality, which has no reality other than Reality. The meeting and touching of the two seas, which are in the self and through which oneness is made manifest as duality, become the meeting and uniting of the male and female, or the father and mother: from these two come pearls and corals.[15]

Duality is the manifestation of oneness whose Self sees Itself in the totality of existence and through it manifests Its divided attributes and names, reveals Its Beauty and the effect of Its creative commandment.

KNOWLEDGE AND BEING

In both cases there exists, although in different ways, the danger of overlooking, neglecting, and denying the possibility of illusion or the power of evil, which is present in the self and outside it—in the world.

In the uncreated intelligence, being and knowledge are one and the same. But, in creation they are separated. Man is the full sign of this: his body indicates being, and his head knowing. They are the outer expression of the separation, or rather divergence, that confirms inwardness or the invisible core. That divergence bears witness to inner oneness, or the heart, which is the "place" of the Intelligence. Thus, knowledge and being are the prolongation or the revelation of that presence of the Intelligence. That presence is two-directional. The reflection of the Intelligence in the self strives toward the edge or the "lower" levels of being.

The totality of existence is not separable from knowledge, so the being constantly endeavors to "ascend" toward knowledge. That is the separation in the self: the tendency toward evil, reproach, and the attainment of Peace. Here too it is possible to recognize the reason love and knowledge are conditions for the balanced suppression and overcoming of evil. The objectivity of the signs in the outer world offers a contrast to the self, which pretends to be preoccupied by the power of deception. And the other way around. The outer horizons attract the self or its inner light prevents it from denying in them the same deceptions that turn it away from the Self.

Those two relations can be revealed also through duty and right. The source of duty is in the self, while right is in something that is outside. Duty is carried out, and right taken. But, there is never duty without an other with a right that is inseparable from it. And the other way around. There is no right that is separable from debt on the other side. Given that both right and debt include division into duality, which neither in love nor in gnosis can deny the origin, intelligence itself is revealed on three levels:

> Intellect, which is One, presents itself in three fundamental aspects—at least insofar as we are situated in the "separative illusion" as is the case for every creature as such—namely, first the divine Intellect, which is Light and pure Act; secondly the cosmic Intellect, which is a receptacle or mirror in relation to God and light in relation to man; and thirdly the human Intellect, which is mirror in relation to both of the foregoing and light in relation to the individual soul; one must be careful, therefore, to distinguish in the Intellect—the divine Intellect excepted—an "uncreated" aspect which is essential and a "created" aspect which is "accidental" or rather "contingent."[16]

Submission transforms the will into love and knowledge. And the self with them and between them resolves its duality in the succession from love to knowledge. Love is between the will and knowledge, and always contains both. It is inseparable from them. And knowledge is centered in what is, and not in what ought to be. And here lies the difference between loving and knowing. Given that man is turned toward God—"wherever you turn there is God's Face!"—to want means to want the Good, and that means to want through the Good or through God; to want thus means to love; and instead of the Good one can say the Beautiful. The one who says he knows says he knows what is; the one who says he knows what is, says, in the final analysis, he is the one who knows—the Self.

God is "Light" before He is "Heat," if it may be so expressed; gnosis "precedes" love, or rather, love "follows" gnosis, since the latter includes love after its own fashion, whereas love is nothing other than the bliss "emanating" from gnosis. One can love something false, without love ceasing to be what it is; but one cannot "know" falsehood in a similar way, that is to say knowledge cannot be under illusion as to its object without ceasing to be what it is; error always implies a privation of knowledge, whereas sin does not imply a privation of will.[17]

Man's appearance speaks of the division of the Intellect into knowing and being. The sign of knowledge is the head, as the body is of being. That division bears witness to the hidden presence of the Intellect of which the sign is the heart. The perfection of that appearance is made manifest in the Praiser. He is permanently present in the human need to be in connection with him, but also absent in the danger of being reduced to an enduring vision in a corporeal image. He is received in all conjectures and dreams and feelings and words, but his beauty is not exhaustible in any solidification. Whenever he appears in a dream, that is he. Satan cannot adopt his form, given that his beauty comes from his connection with the Praised: "He who saw me in a dream," says the Prophet, "in fact saw the truth."[18]

The aspiration that his original beauty be known in the self demands establishing links with this beauty, since it reveals oneness in the divergence of its revelation. The Praiser is the most beautiful uprightness. He is the complete harmony of body and head. His face uncovers the inner world, the center of which is Remembrance, which does not disappear even when he sleeps, nor when he follows, nor when he walks or rides. It is connection with God, so connection with it is liberation from the forgetfulness of God's Face. His wisdom comes from the bringing down of the Word into his heart. And the totality of his form is the prolongation of that and its revelation to other people. "The Prophet is blessed by God and His angels. Bless him, then, you that are true believers, and greet him with a worthy salutation."[19]

That blessing or connection is the disclosure of essential human nature. The measure of closeness to it is the way the Prophet looks, saying: "By Him in Whose Hand is the life of Muhammad, a day would come to you when you would not be able to see me, and the glimpse of my face would be dearer to one than one's own family, one's property and in fact everything."[20]

PROSTRATION

As a whole being, man is ordered from the heart through the brain to the totality of the body. That trinity corresponds to Intellect-consciousness-body or Self-Light-World. The intellect/heart remain hidden, but are, nevertheless, expressed in the duality brain/consciousness and body/world. The presence of the Intellect in the dualities of existence makes possible at every moment, as certainty, the resolution of duality and unification through love and/or knowledge, which is return to the Self or manifestation in It. But, although love appears to be the direct or unifying connection with the Self, it is not possible without knowledge in its active aspect.

> Before being able to "love" it is necessary to "be conscious"; primarily it is light which the sun pours out, rather than heat, as is shown by the visibility of immeasurably distant stars; and to be conscious, in the sense which interests us here, is to fix the heart in the Real, in permanent "remembering" of the Divine. Fear distances one from the world—love brings one near to God; but consciousness "is" already something of its content or its aim; it is true that this remark is also valid for other spiritual modes, but in a less direct way, since intellective consciousness alone surpasses human subjectivity by definition. In a certain sense, loves saves because it includes the whole subject, while

consciousness delivers because it excludes it. (This is not unrelated to the phonetic resemblance of the Latin words *amor* and *mors*. Love, which includes all, is a sort of death, and death, which excludes all, is like losing consciousness in love.)[21]

Just as man's Praise of God is not separable from God's Praise of man, so is man's love for God inseparable from God's Love for man. God's Love is everywhere, given that He created the world in Love, in order to be known. Here love and knowledge are the root, or center, of creation. Love is here identified with the Will. The Self makes Itself known in creation through the Will. Since the Will is not limited, the lover is closer to man than his jugular vein.[22] That closeness means "bringing down" the will to the point of nothingness and ascending to It.[23]

Now the truly sincere lover is the person who changes to (take on) the attributes of the beloved, not someone who brings the beloved down to their own attributes. Don't you see that God, the Truly Real, out of His Love for us, descended to us through His hidden subtle-acts-of-Grace (*altâfuh al-khafiya*), which are appropriate to "us"? (And He does all this out of Love) even though His Majesty and Greatness are exalted far above that. Hence He descended to "smiling happily" with us (as described in another hadith) when we come to His House seeking intimate conversation with Him. And (He descended) to "being filled with joy" at our repenting and returning to Him after we have turned away from Him. And (He descended) to His taking our place in our being hungry and thirsty and sick, to making Himself descend to our level and taking our place whenever one of His servants is ill, so that He said to some of them "I was sick, and you did not visit Me. . . ."

"For these are the fruits of (His) Love when He descended among us." And that is why we said that true sincerity in love makes the lover take on the attributes of the beloved. So the sincere servant (of God) is like that in their love for their Lord, in "taking on the qualities" of His Names. Therefore they take on the (divine) qualities of "being independent" of everything other than God, of "being strong" for God, of "giving bountifully" with God's Hand, and of "safeguarding the Eye of God . . ." because of their love for Him.[24]

When the self wishes to know itself, it seeks the Self. And it finds it only in the world, in the totality of its horizons. But that totality in him is condensed into what he is lacking or into the "home" to which he returns. Only he whom the self sees can be its image. But, the self wants its originator and himself as its image. That is why the attraction of that other, through whom the self sees itself, is irresistible and complete. Before the Other the self, in order to be submissive to that gaze, transforms itself in wholeness, so that all the attributes of the Other, and that means the original nature of the self itself, should be found again or revealed once more.

The one who loves is revealed by the beloved in complete submission in which their separateness ought to disappear. Given that there is no undividedness in existence, prostration is the highest potential of the free will. As it is unattainable in separateness, it is present in remembrance and veiled in forgetfulness. When submission, or prostration, is complete, it includes within itself the whole of multiplicity. Prostration is the denial of duality, since He has no other.

When the lover is completely preoccupied with the closeness of the Beloved, its remembrance too has disappeared. There is only oneness in which everything is taken away in an instant that is eternity. Return to the multitude can bear witness to two things—the world as a place of disclosure instead of Him Who discloses Himself, which is the denial of oneness and seeing the signs as the Signified, or turning away through remembrance and cleansing to Him Who does not accept any other and Who is the friend of everything that is in existence.

When a man approaches that prostration, he touches the world, which is in its entirety the place of prostration. Then, the self, in which his satisfaction and satisfaction with him have once again become his highest nature, clearly refracts the totality of existence—both the heavens and the earth—into their collectedness in serene humanity. The highest closeness of the male and the female, which appears in an instant as the manifestation of oneness, becomes the presence of indivisibility between their revelation in the world and in man.

The individual is always opposite God's Face. If God's Face is complete Reality, then man can be only His image. Unity is the disappearance of the image in the Face. That is returning of the duality to oneness. Prostration is that return, just as it is also the union of the male and the female.

Creation or manifestation is the descent of the first toward the last, while oneness remains the first and the last. That descent takes place in the six days of creation. In each new day the descent is closer to man, the first intention and last attainment of all creation. Man is at the end or in the depths. Everything that is divided from the first to the sixth day is gathered together in man. He is, therefore, the intention at the beginning and the revelation at the end. Man is therefore capable of returning at will through the whole of creation and its totality in him to complete serenity, and thus to see the first and the last things in himself and to be His pure image. Acceptance of that position at the end and in the depths is serenity. In his highest potential man is the serene one who reflects Peace. The relation between him as serene and the Self as Peace is soothing. And that is the meaning of the Prophet's bidding to say "I am commanded to be the first of those who shall submit to Him." [25] And prostration is the full expression of that serenity. Through it the fullness of creation is carried into the seventh day, or serenity, into being with the seven signs or the seven supports, in the manifestation of Peace as the beginning and as the end.

The offering of the self as clothing to the other and accepting the other as one's clothing is serenity or a return to Peace. [26]

Remembrance

Man is in the world and opposite it. Accepting submission, which is the way of existence of that opposite world, means the confirmation of the human nature of the created one. And that nature demands a Creator. One seeks the other. The Creator manifests Himself in the created one who is, thus, the revelation of His Words. Without the created one the Word is hidden, unrevealed, and undivided. It is only an unarticulated name.

Man's submission or serenity becomes the "transcription" of that hiddenness into revelation, just as the world is. And man can express it, thus disclosing himself, the world and God. In that submission, in which man makes manifest all God's names, the will remains free. And there remains also the sense of separateness from Him to Whom one submits. He is incomparable and similar to nothing, while man wishes to be close to Him and for Him to see Himself in and through him.

Complete serenity means also complete closeness. And this means the disappearance of the separation of the self between nothingness as its ultimate impossibility and Peace as unity. Since no state of the self outside complete Peace is complete submission either, it is, with regard to the free will, between remembrance and forgetting. The fullness of submission would be the fullness of remembrance. And the other way around—the fullness of forgetfulness would be contradiction of the Creator. And that is not possible.

Submission is entry into the order of the world in order that its borders and paths should be confirmed. For paths and borders manifest signs. But they speak of the truth, which is one, although it is manifested in the countless multiplicity of phenomena. The reasonable expression of that is sobriety. But derangement and the consequent impossibility of inclusion into sensible speech, which is the harmonized relation of the self and the world, are nothing other than forgetfulness and drunkenness. And the interrelation between the Creator and the creature is the love of the first for the other. That first gives existence to the other out of His love to be known. He wishes to see Himself through that other, and so places him in His debt through his creation.

That debt of creation may be repaid only in sober concentration on it and turning toward Him to Whom it should be repaid. That is why submission (*islam*) is the first condition of human existence. This is humankind's orientation. But that orientation is only the condition for maintaining and strengthening remembrance in its aim—seeing God's Face as oneness revealed in multiplicity: "Prayer forbids indecency and dishonor, God's remembrance is greater."[27] This seeing makes possible recognition in the world of the attributes of power, ruling, greatness, administration, righteousness, knowledge, and the like. They are gathered together in the Throne of the Ruler of all existence.

Remembrance directs one toward the Throne. And He Who has infinite power, Whom the directed one remembers, does not cease to be a source of fear, since He is distant and incomparable with anything. Here remembrance is revealed as fear. But, directedness and moving toward Him make possible also closeness. And when it is attained, it becomes clear that both closeness and distance, and love and fear, are the reality of human existence. In closeness remembrance is transformed into security.

Living in the world and society demands knowing and maintaining order. And that requires answers to the questions of "how?" which, along with the threat of punishment, are posed by the Almighty.

Transgression of those commandments brings down wrath and punishment. But closeness, which is attained through submission, comes to know and experience Mercy, Mildness, and Tenderness. Thus enslavement is transformed into loving. And love requires closeness. That is the expectation that the lover sees the beloved as most beautiful to him. He who loves sees himself through the beloved and expects that what he sees will be the most beautiful.

But the lover and the beloved are separate. All weariness or turning away in that looking leads to negligence and forgetfulness. And here too the Praiser is the most beautiful example:

> His own heart did not deny his vision.
> How can you, then, question what he sees?
> He beheld him once again by the sidra tree, beyond which
> no one may pass. (Near it is the Garden of Repose.)
> When that tree was covered with what covered it, his eyes
> did not wander, nor did they turn aside: for he saw
> some of his Lord's greatest signs.[28]

And since human nature does not accept separateness, negligence and forgetfulness are accompanied by pain. Through it, as in a flash, the human state is made manifest. Out of forgetfulness and pain comes drunkenness. They are the undirectedness and sin that summon one to turn toward the aim. And that is the content of human nature, as the Prophet says: "If you were not to commit sin, God would sweep you out of existence and He would replace you by those people who would commit sin and seek forgiveness from God, and He would have pardoned them."[29] But that renewed remembrance and directedness demand prayer and sober speech: "Believers, do not approach your prayers when you are drunk, but wait till you can grasp the meaning of your words."[30]

Speaking is division, where the divided and the revealed bear witness to the united and the secret. Reasonable speech, consequently, is the confirmation of the oneness that is manifest in the multitude. Distance is the territory of duality, multiplicity, division, right and wrong, commandment and prohibition, good and evil—of what is expressed in the law. While closeness is the territory of oneness, undividedness, sameness, unity. They correspond to Mercy, tenderness, and gentleness. Thus, man lives in distance and closeness, and law and love.

It is possible to turn to one's Creator by each of these paths, but never by denying the duality of one's nature. The imbalance of these two expressions of oneness is revealed as forgetfulness and drunkenness. In them it is not possible to recognize that man is in every moment in a different place. The moment imposes this change, and the place receives it. And that is why his sobriety is necessary, for wherever he finds himself, there is the mosque, the place of prostration through which the one who prays connects himself to the prostration of everything in existence.

The demand to turn to the inviolable temple is an invitation to bring into harmony the seeing of signs in the horizons with seeing signs in the self, for they are two sides of the confirmation of the truth. And that is why the earth is pure for the one who prays, knowing that the invitation to cleanse the inviolable mosque means the commandment to cleanse one's heart for the sake of its reflection of the purity of the worlds. But God's Mercy is the beginning and the end, for His Mercy surpasses His wrath.

Both remembrance and forgetting are between power and beauty as two inseparable expressions of oneness. The Intellect is at the height of creation: the totality of creation is the descent from it or its divergence. The ultimate point of that descent is man. In him is gathered the totality of separation or the revealed Divine names. He is, thus, the image that has been brought out of potential into existence. Through man, the Intellect becomes active in the world. By accepting submission, man is the sum of everything existing. And by turning to the first Intellect, he returns to his nature full of the first things, whereby through submission he acknowledges and makes manifest distance and power, and through his return closeness and beauty.

When he demands to be exempt from power and submission to it, he joins his self to the Divine Self, and thus denies his nature as created. And the self that wishes for closeness without submission and fear expresses lust and insatiability, and thus denies that God remembers those who remember Him.[31] Thus is division in the self—the self that leads toward evil, the self that reprimands itself, and the self at peace—submitted to one of the expressions of duality, power or beauty, and not the self at peace. In that way the male and the female principle are separated from oneness and strengthen the self as opposition to the Self.

The Self at Peace

In the preceding reflections, six doors were knocked on for the sake of finding an answer to the question of love.[1] Whenever the path toward one of them led to the right, whether it was open or remained closed, the "here and now" of the traveling self lay between that orientation and what remained to the left. It was the same when the direction toward that door or what lay behind it led straight: the "here and now" of the self remained between that and what was left behind. But two paths and two doors remained impossible—the one leading vertically upward and the one leading steeply down.

And the "here and now" of the human self is revealed as clearly divided in that impossibility that determines it more than any one of the paths on the surface of the earth. It is the same in potential and impossibility. And, since it is not manifested in potential, what remains is impossibility. By conquering that, one would be transformed into the other. The potential would, really, become the way it would seem if it were drawn out of the higher, if the visible were simply the revelation of the invisible. Through the confirmation of the signs in himself and in the horizons, a man would open the door of heaven. And with that his dividedness would be resolved. And that dividedness is in the "here and now" of his self. It is between darkness, whose fullness is nothingness, and light, whose fullness is the treasury of all things.

Darkness is always beneath light. The seventy thousand veils of darkness and light on God's Face correspond to a different expression, the world of darkness and the world of light. Only with light does the relationship of the two remain the manifestation of the One. Without light the worlds are nothing. Everything is created with it and returns to it. The reason for creation is knowledge, which reaches its perfection in the worlds. The worlds as a whole make manifest the names of the Creator, and man does the same, for in himself he encompasses all phenomena:

> The Reality wanted to see the essences of His Most Beautiful Names or, to put it another way, to see His own Essence, in an all-inclusive object encompassing the whole (divine) Command, which, qualified by existence, would reveal to Him His own mystery. For the seeing of a thing, itself, by itself, is not the same as its seeing itself in another, as it were in a mirror; for it appears to itself in a form that is invested by the location of the vision by that which would only appear to it given the existence of the location and its (the location's) self-disclosure to it.[2]

If all the worlds are seventy thousand veils of light and darkness or, put differently, light and dark, the first corresponds to the Self, which rules, and the second to the territory of that rule. The hiddenness of the first is made manifest in the visibility of the second. So it is in the human self. It is divided between its extremes in darkness and light, evil and good. Both those directions belong to it, and they are in tension.

The tendency downward, toward darkness or evil, is the presence of the self that leads to evil. But no state is without Reality or light. And that is the cause of the lack of serenity of the self in evil. In the span of that divergence the self that reproaches itself is always present. Those two sides of one and the same self, which are in a constant, great war one against the other, reflect divergence. And only unity is victory. Unity can, in the final outcome, belong only to Reality. And that is why the only path of the human "here and now" is the one that leads to that victory and return. That is the one the Almighty summons us to:

O serene soul! Return to your Lord,
joyful and pleasing in His sight.[3]

Notes

1. The word in the original (*jastvo*) means literally "I-ness." Later in the text it is contrasted with "you-ness" (*tistvo*) and "he-ness" (*onstvo*). The human "I-ness" is also contrasted with Divine "I-ness," which is printed with a capital initial letter. Since such expressions are impossible in English, I have opted for "self" (and "Self") in the body of the text. On the other hand, the final section, which would be "the 'self' at peace," is translated by Arthur J. Arberry (in *The Koran Interpreted*) as "the soul at peace" and by N. J. Dawood (in *The Koran*, the Penguin Classics translation) as "serene soul." I have opted for "the soul at peace." But in the rest of the text, I have also felt it necessary to maintain a distinction between "self" (*jastvo*) and "soul" (*duša*). Trans.

FIRST DOOR
The Impossibility of Definition

1. Ibn al-'Arabi, *al-Futūhāt al-makkiyya* 2:325.13. Quotation from Chittick, "The Divine Roots of Human Love," 57.

2. Qur'an 1:6–7. Given that this discussion is written in the traditional view, the most frequent quotations are from the Qur'an ("Teachings"), and the Torah, Psalms, Gospels, and texts that are connected with them. All translations of parts of these works are taken from *The Koran*, translated with notes by N. J. Dawood; Arthur J. Arberry, *The Koran Interpreted*; and *The Thompson Chain-Reference Bible: King James Version*.

3. Schuon, *Form and Substance in the Religions*, 245.

4. Samnûn is a famous spiritual teacher from Iraq. For details about him, see al-Sulami, *Tabaqât al-sufiyya*, 195–99.

5. Kubra, *Les éclosions de la beauté et les parfums de la majesté*, 165; see idem, *La pratique du soufisme: Quatorze petits traits,* 79. Thus, the main contradiction with which love must come into contact is the one between life and death. "To love life as it really is," says Thomas Merton, "means to accept it in its total reality, which includes death; to accept not only the *idea* of death but also those acts which anticipate death, in the offering and giving of ourselves." (Merton, preface to *Love*, by Cardenal, 16.)

6. In Arberry, the quotation is "He is God, One, God, the Everlasting Refuge," with "refuge" being the translation of the word given in this text as "Flow." *Translator's note.*

7. Qur'an 112:1–4.

8. Ibid. 51:49.

9. Ibid. 53:45. That statement about the male and the female as a created duality is the key to opening the question of God's oneness. Man addresses God out of language as one of His signs (ibid. 30:22). Grammatical gender in every language should, therefore, be understood as addressing oneness out of the created multiplicity which makes it manifest. Each of these addresses to God includes the dualities of everything that has been created, but also the incomparability and unlikeness of everything to do with the Creator. If the forms "He," "Him," "to Him," etc., included gender, the necessary consequence of this would be duality or "having a companion, male or female," and birth and being born. But He/She denies such a possibility, offering that as the greatest principle (ibid. 6:163). That is why He/She is the Only One. The male and the female are a duality, and that means also createdness, while He/She is not created nor gives birth nor is born. Every understanding of addressing God as male includes the idea that woman, and necessarily also a child, is thus assigned to Him. This denies His oneness, so consequently also the simultaneity of distance from everything that is created and closeness to Him. That is why the statements in the Teaching are comprehensible: "Creator of the heavens and the earth. How should He have a son, when He had no consort?" (ibid. 6:101). "He (exalted be the glory of our Lord!) has taken no consort, nor has He begotten any children" (ibid. 72:3).

10. Ibid. 2:187.

11. Bukhari, *Sahih*, 9:381. The verb *kān* ("was") is translated as "is" given that when it refers to God it cannot have any temporal meaning. See Murata, *The Tao of Islam*, 333 n 4.

12. Quoted from Schuon, *Stations of Wisdom*, 57.

13. See Qur'an 2:31.

14. In the original, the second term (*ljubiti*) means "to love," but it may also mean "to kiss." The neatness of the original is thus inevitably lost in this attempt at translating the author's intention. *Translator's note.*

15. See Qur'an 38:75
16. In verse 51:50 of the Qur'an God stresses the conclusion of the contention about the duality of everything created: "Therefore seek God."

SECOND DOOR
Will

1. Qur'an 33:72.
2. Genesis 1:26. This affirmation is of decisive importance in the intellectual heritage of the Prophet Muhammed. It is connected with his statement "God created Adam in His own image." (Muslim, *Sahih* 4:1378.) See, also, Chittick, *The Sufi Path of Knowledge*, 399 n. 4.
3. Bukhari, *Sahih* 8:336.
4. Ibn al-'Arabi, *al-Futūhāt al-makkiyya* 2:298.29.
5. Qur'an 30:21.
6. See ibid. 7:156.
7. Ibid. 7:19–20.
8. The Teaching is the Qur'an. *Translator's note.*
9. See Qur'an 5:33 and the interpretation in Asad, *The Message of the Qur'an*, 148–49.
10. The First Epistle of Paul to the Corinthians 13:11–12.
11. Qur'an 21:30.
12. Ibid. 7:189.
13. See ibid. 41:11.
14. Ibid. 7:172.
15. Muslim, *Sahih* 4:1397.
16. Schuon, *Stations of Wisdom*, 148.
17. Schuon, *Form and Substance in the Religions*, 245.
18. Qur'an 90:8–17. The emphasis on caring for the poor as a condition of ascendance shows that the fulfillment of duty to God is complete if it comes from the free will, for the attraction of Peace and its attainment excludes compulsion, unlike the opposite force of the lower world. The fulfillment of duty to the poor person, who is helpless, is directing the will toward God as Peace, so that it should respond, as Jesus too says in the Gospels (Luke 14:13–14): "But when thou makest a feast, call the poor, the maimed, the lame, the blind! And thou shalt be blessed; for they cannot recompense thee: for thou shalt be recompensed at the resurrection of the just."
19. Majlisī, *Bihār al-anwār* 1:117.

THIRD DOOR
Love

1. Luke 2:14.
2. See Qur'an 12:53.

3. Here "the Praiser" is the translation of the Arabic name "Muhammad." It is worth explaining the reason for this translation in the active form instead of the passive ("the Praised"), which would be literal. The nature of being Praised in this exposition is the manifestation of the Divine name "the Praiser." Thus, the relation between man as Praised and God as the Praiser is Grace. And Grace belongs to God. Accepting Grace and making it manifest in himself, the Praised is also the Praiser, for what he has accepted into his inner being he radiates out through his outer being. Thus, being the Praiser, he is through Grace in a relationship with God as the Praised. And that is a way of making manifest God's name "Praiser/ Praised." Comparable with this is also his nature of the shining candle. He has accepted light—and God is the light of the heavens and the earth!—and radiates it as his true nature. Connecting that with the testimony that there is no god other than God, it is possible to say that there is no praiser other than the Praiser, nor praised other than the Praised. The proposed translation would correspond to the old Bosnian name "Hval," which has the same sound as the feminine gender noun *hval*. That name encompasses both Muhammad's natures, the receiving and the giving, the passive and the active.

4. This is an explicit proclamation in the Psalms, the Gospels, and the Teaching. See, for example, Psalms 147:14; John 14:27; and Qur'an 59:23.

5. The Arabic noun *islam* ("submission," "pacifying") has the same verbal root as the noun *salam* ("peace") and *muslim* ("who is comforted"/ "pacified").

6. Ibn al-'Arabi, *al-Futūhāt al-makkiyya*, 2:399.28. For more about this saying, see Chittick, *The Sufi Path of Knowledge*, 250. Given the key content of this saying, according to which God through His messenger Muhammed speaks about love as the root of creation, it is worth emphasizing that this is also a Christian viewpoint. See, for example, Max Scheler, "Love and Knowledge," 147–65 in *On Feeling, Knowing, and Valuing*.

7. The term given in the original is *dug*, the first meaning of which is "debt." It is translated in the versions of the Qur'an I have consulted as "faith" or "religion." But where the meaning "debt" is essential to the sense of this text, I have retained that meaning. *Translator's note.*

8. Qur'an 30:30.

9. Tabarsi, *Mishkat ul-Anwar fi Ghurar il-Akhbar*, 304.

10. Ibid.

11. The Messenger says that the mutual naming of Peace is a condition of love. (See Tabarsi, *Mishkat ul-Anwar fi Ghurar il-Akhbar*, 310.)

12. Perry, *A Treasury of Traditional Wisdom*, 164.

13. Muslim, *Sahih* 1:53.

14. Schuon, *Sprititual Perspectives and Human Facts*, 220.

15. See Qur'an 90:8–17.

16. The difference between "contemplation" and "concentration" must be emphasized.

17. The Prophet says: "God is beautiful and He loves beauty" (Muslim, *Sahih* 1:53).

18. See Qur'an 36:40.

19. Schuon, *Stations of Wisdom*, 149.

20. See Qur'an 6:103.

21. See Bukhari, *Sahih* 9:482.

22. "Knock, and it shall be opened unto you" (Matthew 7:7.)

23. "Seek and ye shall find" (ibid.).

24. The Almighty says in the Teaching (Qur'an 40:60): "Call upon me and I will answer you."

25. Ibid. 13:28.

26. Ibid. 28:88.

27. Schuon, *Stations of Wisdom*, 150.

28. God says: "I was hungry, but you did not feed Me; I was thirsty, but you did not give me to drink; I was ill, but you did not visit Me." This saying is often quoted by Ibn 'Arabi in his work *al-Futūhāt al-makkiyya*. A variation on it occurs in Muslim, *Sahih* 4:1363. (See Graham, *Divine Word and Prophetic Word in Early Islam*, 179–80; and Chittick, *The Sufi Path of Knowledge*, 392 n. 33.) The statement is comparable to that in Matthew 25:41–45.

29. Qur'an 17:109.

30. Ibid. 28:70.

31. Ibn Maja, *al-Sunan: Muqaddima*, 13. On this tradition see Ghazali, *The Niche of Lights,* 44–53.

32. Qur'an 15:21.

33. Genesis 1:2.

34. See Gril, "There Is No Word in the World That Does Not Indicate His Praise," 31–43.

35. See Qur'an 57:4.

36. Muslim, *Sahih* 1:373.

37. Rumi, *The Mathnawi* 6:4303–4.

38. Schimmel, *The Triumphal Sun*, 231.

39. See Bukhari, *Sahih* 4:385–86.

40. Zayn al-'Abidin, *The Psalms of Islam,* 41. Envy is the identification of the place of revelation of love with itself. That is impurity, so it is understandable that St. Maximos the Confessor says: "If we detect any trace of hatred in our hearts against any man whatsoever for committing any fault, we are utterly estranged from love for God, since love for God absolutely precludes us from hating any man" (*The Philocalia* 2:54).

FOURTH DOOR
Toward Peace

1. The term "All-loving," from the Arberry translation of the Qur'an, is used in the title of this section because it conveys the topic of this chapter

more clearly than the Dawood translation of "benignant," in the quotation given at the end of the first paragraph. *Translator's note.*

2. Of this well-known and often quoted holy saying, Ibn al-'Arabi says: "That is sound on the basis of unveiling, but not established by way of transmission" (*al-Futūhāt al-makkiyya* 2:399.28).

3. Qur'an 85:14.

4. Ibid. 7:172–73.

5. Ibid. 2:115.

6. Muslim, *Sahih* 4:1481.

7. See Muslim, *Sahih* 4:1397.

8. See Qur'an 3:31. That formulation "God will love those who love Him and follow His Emissary" may be recognized in the Praiser's pronouncement "I am most akin to the son of Mary among the whole of mankind and the prophets are of different mothers, but of one religion. And no Prophet was raised between me and him" (Muslim, *Sahih* 4:1260). Following the Messenger is the renewal and maintenance of the original connection with God, as Jesus too says: "He that loveth father or mother more than me, is not worthy of me. And he that loveth son or daughter more than me is not worthy of me. And he that taketh not his cross, and followeth after me, is not worthy of me. He that findeth his life shall lose it: and who that loseth his life for my sake shall find it" (Matthew, 10:37–39). "None of You is a believer," says the Praiser, "till I am dearer to him than his child, his father and the whole of mankind" (Muslim, *Sahih* 1:31). That connection with the Messenger is the love of man and God. It is always the same—"the messengers are of different mothers but of one religion."

9. Qur'an 2:222.

10. Ibid. 3:76.

11. Ibid. 3:134.

12. Ibid. 3:146.

13. Ibid. 19:96.

14. Ibid. 5:54.

15. See Qur'an 14:3.

16. See Qur'an 2:165.

17. See Qur'an 89:20.

18. See Qur'an 29:25.

19. Qur'an 29:25.

20. See Qur'an 45:13.

21. Ibn al-'Arabi, *al-Futūhāt al-makkiyya* 1:139.10.

22. See Qur'an 17:23–24.

23. Qur'an 3:118.

24. See Qur'an 2:190.

25. See Qur'an 2:205 and 5:64.

26. See Qur'an 2:276.

27. See Qur'an 3:57.
28. See Qur'an 4:36 and 16:23.
29. See Qur'an 4:107.
30. See Qur'an 5:87.
31. See Qur'an 6:141.
32. See Qur'an 30:45.
33. Qur'an 38:32.
34. Ibid. 3:92.
35. Ibid. 59:9.
36. Ibid. 3:14.
37. Ibid. 2:177.
38. Ghazali, *Ihyā' ulūm al-dīn*, 2:2.1.
39. Qur'an 22:18.
40. See Qur'an 112:4.
41. See Qur'an 42:11.
42. See Qur'an 50:16.
43. See Qur'an 57:4.
44. See Qur'an 2:115.
45. Ibn al-'Arabi, *Inshâ al-dawā'ir*, in *Kleine Schriften des Ibn al-'Arabi*, 1–40, 21.
46. Murata, *The Tao of Islam*, 17.
47. See Tirmidhi, "Sufi Psychological Treatise," 244–46.
48. Qunawi, *Miftah al-ghayb*, 163.
49. Qur'an 5:116.
50. Ibid. 30:7.
51. In the original text, the terms for "otherness" are formed from the personal pronouns "you" ("you-ness") and "he" ("he-ness"), which complement the term translated in this text as "self" ("I-ness"). *Translator's note.*
52. See Qur'an 40:7.
53. Qur'an 42:23.
54. "God is All-compassionate, All-loving" (Qur'an 11:90 and 85:14).
55. See Qur'an 41:34.
56. Qur'an 60:7.
57. Matthew 22:37–40.
58. Qur'an 16:40.

FIFTH DOOR
Following

1. Qur'an 27:93.
2. Ibid. 33:21.
3. Ibid. 68:4.

4. Ibid. 33:46.
5. Ibid, 21:107.
6. John 8:50–51.
7. Ibid. 8:54.
8. Ibid. 10:17–18
9. Ibid. 12:25–26.
10. Ibid. 13:34–35.
11. Luke 10:27.
12. Qur'an 3:31.
13. Schuon, *Stations of Wisdom*, 59.
14. Qur'an 33:6. Here I have given the translation from Arberry, since the Dawood translation of this verse is "The Prophet has a greater claim on the faithful than they have on each other." But the use of the term "self" is important for the sense of this paragraph. *Translator's note.*
15. Luke 14:26. Translations of "and does not hate" as "and prefers" are more frequent.
16. Matthew 16:24.
17. See Muslim, *Sahih* 1:31.
18. See Bukhari, *Sahih* 4:140.
19. Hanbal, *al-Musnad* 1:368.
20. See Luke 14:26.
21. See Matthew 5:44.
22. See Qur'an 41:34.
23. See Leviticus 19:18 and Matthew 22:39.
24. See Qur'an 33:6.
25. Qur'an 45:23.
26. Ibid. 2:165.
27. Ibid. 6:151.
28. Ibid. 102:1–3.
29. On one occasion, the Prophet said to his companions: "We have returned from the Lesser Holy War to the Greater Holy War." And when one of them asked: "What is the Greater Holy War, O Messenger of God?" He answered: "The war against the soul!" (Quoted in Khâtib al-Baghdâdî, *Târîkh Baghdâd,* 493, 523.)
30. Qur'an 2:150.
31. Ibid. 7:156.
32. Ibid. 47:38.
33. See Qur'an 33:72.
34. See Qur'an 113:2–5.
35. See Muslim, *Sahih* 4:1481.
36. See Qur'an 2:268.
37. Bukhari, *Sahih* 8:336–37.
38. Variations of this saying are found in al-Nasā'i, *al-Sunan: 'Ishrat al-Nisā'*, 1; Hanbal, *al-Musnad* 3:128, 199, 285; the variation given here

comes from Ghazali, *Ihyā' 'ulūm al-dīn* 2:2.1. (See Murata, *The Tao of Islam*, 345 n. 43.)

39. The prayer here is the translation of the Arabic word *salat* ("compulsory bowing down"). That bowing includes entry into a dedicated state, praise, and glorification; remembrance and prayer. Although the etymology of this concept is obscure, it is possible to find in it a connection with the meanings "to raise up," "to elevate," "to emphasize," "to support," "to repeat," "to link," etc. Encompassing all these semantic possibilities, it is worth emphasizing that *salat* confirms man's position in the dividedness between the lower and the higher in the multitude of levels of existence and directedness toward the principle of oneness. It is also worth mentioning that the traditional interpreters of this saying of the Prophet's have recognized and researched the "aroma" (otherwise often connected with femaleness and closeness) as a masculine noun between "woman" and "prayer" as feminine nouns. The mystery of that relationship is an inexhaustible stimulus to Sufi discourse. On this see Schimmel, *My Soul Is a Woman*, 33.

40. Qur'an 57:4.

41. Exodus 20:5. It is possible to read this statement also as a variation of the Qur'an's message (4:48): "God will not forgive those who serve other gods beside Him." The Prophet says: "You people are astonished at Sa'd's jealousy. By God, I am more jealous than he, and God is more jealous than I, and because of God's jealousy, He has made unlawful shameful deeds and sins done in open and in secret" (Bukhari, *Sahih* 9:378–79). On this Divine jealousy as nonacceptance of a Reality beyond His see more in the interpretations of Ibn al-'Arabi (Chittick, *The Sufi Path of Knowledge*, 295). This statement of the Prophet's is the core of the tale "The Interpretation of the Pronouncement of Hakim" in *The Mathnavi*. (See Rumi, *The Mathnawi* 2:96–99.)

42. See Qur'an 5:54.

43. Pfeiffer, *Meister Eckhart* 1:114.

44. Bukhari, *Sahih* 8:372.

45. See Qur'an 7:20–21 and 20:120–21.

SIXTH DOOR
Knowledge

1. Qur'an 29:46.
2. Ibid. 20:14.
3. See 'Ali ibn Ebi Talib, *Nahjul Balagha.* 334.
4. Qur'an 41:19–23.
5. Ibid. 41:34.
6. Ibid. 39:23.
7. Muslim, *Sahih* 1:113.

8. The Greek concept *orgasmos* comes from *organ* ("to swell") and indicates "fierce rapture," "great excitement," and, particularly, "the climax of coupling in the sexual act." The concept "sex" may be connected with the old French *sexe* from the Latin *sexus,* earlier *secus* from *secare* ("to cut off," "separate"). That sense is comprehensible because oneness is revealed in duality—active and passive, male and female, etc. But, it is worth knowing also the connection of that concept with the Latin *sex* ("six") given that every detail is revealed in its six spatial measures, which start from oneness and return to it as their reality. Sex is the central content of marriage as the frame for human realization, or fulfillment of the Debt. "When a slave marries," says the Prophet, "he has fulfilled half of the Debt, and let him be aware of God for the second half." (This saying is quoted, with slight differences, also by Tabarāni and Baghdâdî. See Sakhawi, *Al-Maqasid al-Hasana fi Bayan min al-Ahadith al-Mushtahira 'ala al-Sunna* 407, saying no. 1098.)

9. The Almighty announces in the Teaching: "Are the disbelievers unaware that the heavens and the earth were but one solid mass which We tore asunder, and that We made every living thing from water?" (Qur'an 21:30). "It was He who created man from water, and gave him kindred of blood and of marriage" (ibid. 25:54).

10. The Merciful speaks in the Teaching about man's creation from a water drop (see, for example, ibid. 18:37), and in that drop are contained the possibilities that are revealed in the totality of human life. Turning toward that creation is an invitation to the self: "Recite in the name of your Lord who created—created man from clots of blood" (ibid. 96:1–2).

11. Ibn al-'Arabi, *al-Futūhāt al-makkiyya* 2:304.19.

12. Ibid. 2:327. See also Addas, "The Experience and Doctrine of Love in Ibn 'Arabi," 36.

13. Schuon, *Gnosis*, 65.

14. Qur'an 25:53.

15. See Qur'an 55:22.

16. Schuon, *Gnosis*, 65–66.

17. Ibid., 70.

18. Muslim, *Sahih* 4:1225.

19. Qur'an 33:56.

20. Muslim, *Sahih* 4:1260.

21. Schuon, *Gnosis*, 84–85.

22. See Qur'an 50:16.

23. See Qur'an 58:7.

24. Ibn al-'Arabi, *al-Futūhāt al-makkiyya* 2:276, 2:596. (Quoted from Morris, "Seeking God's Face," 27–28.)

25. Qur'an 39:12.

26. See Qur'an 30:21.

27. Qur'an 29:45.
28. Ibid. 53:11–18.
29. Muslim, *Sahih* 4:1436.
30. Qur'an 4:43.
31. See Qur'an 2:152.

THE SOUL AT PEACE

1. The translation given by Dawood for the phrase that serves as the title to this chapter is "the serene soul," but it seemed important to retain the term "self" for the sense of this passage. *Translator's note.*
2. Ibn al-'Arabi, *The Bazels of Wisdom*, 50.
3. Qur'an 89:27–28.

Bibliography

Abu Dā'ūd al-Sidjistānī. *al-Sunan*. Cairo: Mustafā al-Bābi al-Halabī, 1952.

Addas, Claude. "The Experience and Doctrine of Love in Ibn 'Arabi." *Journal of the Muhyiddin Ibn 'Arabi Society* 32 (2002): 25–44.

'Ali ibn Ebi Talib, Imam. *Nahjul Balagha: Sermons, Letters and Sayings of Imam Ali*, Qum: Ansariyan Publications, 1989.

Arberry, Arthur J. *The Koran Interpreted*. London: Allen & Unwin, 1980.

Asad, Muhammad. *The Message of the Qur'an*. Gibraltar: Dar al-Andalus, 1980.

Baghdâdî, Khâtib al-. *Târîkh Baghdâd*. 13 vols, Cairo: Maktaba al-Khânjî, 1349.

Bukhari, Imam al-. *Sahih al-Bukhari*. Translated by Muhammad Muhsin Khan. 9 vols. Beirut: Dar al Arabia, 1985.

Cardenal, Ernesto. *Love*. London: Search Press, 1974.

Chittick, William C. "The Divine Roots of Human Love." *Journal of the Muhyiddin Ibn 'Arabi Society* 17 (1995): 55–78.

———. *The Sufi Path of Knowledge: Ibn al-Arabi's Metaphysics of Imagination*. New York: State University of New York Press, 1989.

Ghazālī, Muhammad al-. *Ihyā' 'ūlum al-dīn*. Cairo: Matba'at al-'Amirat al-Sharafiyya, 1908–9.

———. *The Niche of Lights*. Translated by David Buchman. Provo, Utah: Brigham Young University Press, 1998.

Graham, William A. *Divine Word and Prophetic Word in Early Islam*. The Hague: Mouton, 1997.

Gril, Denis. "There Is No Word in the World That Does Not Indicate His Praise." *Journal of the Muhyiddin Ibn 'Arabi Society* 21 (1997): 31–43.

Hanbal, Ahmad ibn. *al-Musnad*. Beirut: Dâr Sadir, n.d.

Ibn al-'Arabi. *The Bazels of Wisdom*. Translated and with an introduction by R. W. J. Austin. New York: Paulist Press, 1980.

————. *al-Futūhāt al-makkiyya.* Cairo, 1911. (Reprint, Cairo: Al-Hay'at al-Misriyyat al-Amma li l'Kitab, 1972; reprint, Beirut: Dâr Sadir, n.d.)

————. *Inshâ' al-dawā'ir,* in *Kleine Schriften des Ibn al-'Arabi.* Edited by Henrik S. Nyberg. Leiden: E. J. Brill, 1919.

Ibn Maja, Abu 'Abd Allah Muhammad. *al-Sunan.* Cairo: Dar Ihya' al-Kutub al-Arabiyya, 1952.

The Koran. Translated with notes by N. J. Dawood. London: Penguin Books, 2003.

Kubra, Najm al-din. *Les éclosions de la beauté et les parfums de la majesté.* Nîmes: L'Éclat, 2001.

————. *La pratique du soufisme: Quatorze petits traits.* Translated by Paul Ballanfat. Nîmes: L'Éclat, 2002.

Kulenović, Skender. *Soneti.* Vol. 2. Novi Sad: Matica srpska, 1974.

Lings, Martin. *Muhammad: His Life Based on the Earliest Sources.* London: Allen & Unwin, 1988.

Majlisī, Muhammad Baqir. *Bihār al-anwār.* Beirut: Mu'assat al-Wafa', 1983.

Morris, James W. "Seeking God's Face: Ibn 'Arabi on Right Action and Theophanic Vision." *Journal of the Muhyiddin Ibn 'Arabi Society* 17 (1995): 1–39.

Murata, Sachiko. *The Tao of Islam: A Sourcebook on Gender Relationship in Islamic Thought.* Albany: State University of New York Press, 1992.

Muslim, Imam. *Sahih Muslim.* Translated by 'Abdul Hamid Siddiqi. 4 vols. Riyadh: International Islamic Publishing House, n.d.

Nasā'i, Abū 'Abd al Rahmān al-. *al-Sunan.* Beirut: Dar Ihya' al-Turath al-Arabi, 1929–30.

Perry, Whitall N. *A Treasury of Traditional Wisdom.* Cambridge, England: Quinta Essentia, 1991.

Pfeiffer, Franz. *Meister Eckhart.* Translated by C. de B. Evans. London: John M. Watkins, 1924.

The Philocalia: The Complete Text. 2 vols. Collected by St. Nikodimos of the Holy Mountain and St. Makarios of Corinth. Translated by G. E. H. Palmer, Philip Sherrard, and Kallistos Ware. London: Faber & Faber, 1981.

Qūnawī, Sadr al-Dīn al-. *Miftāh al-ghayb.* Printed in the margin of *Misbāh al-ins bayn al-ma'qul wa'l-mangul fi sharh Miftāh ghayb al-jam' wa'l-wujūd,* by Shams al-Dīn Muhammad al-Fanārī. Tehran: Ahmad Shīrāzī, 1905.

Rumi, Jalal al-Din. *The Mathnawi.* Edited and translated by Reynold A. Nicholson. London: Luzac, 1925–40.

Sakhawi, Shams al-Din Abu al-Khayr Muhammad al-. *Al-Maqasid al-Hasana fi Bayan min al-Ahadith al-Mushtahira 'ala al-Sunna.* Cairo: Maktab al-Khanji, 1991.

Scheler, Max. *On Feeling, Knowing, and Valuing*. Chicago: University of Chicago Press, 1992.

Schimmel, Annemarie. *My Soul Is a Woman: The Feminine in Islam*. Translated by Susan H. Ray. New York: Continuum International, 1997.

———. *The Triumphal Sun: A Study of the Works of Jalaloddin Rumi*. London: Fine Books, 1978.

Schuon, Frithjof. *Form and Substance in the Religions*. Bloomington, IN: World Wisdom Books, 2002.

———. *Gnosis: Divine Wisdom*. Middlesex: Perennial Books, 1990.

———. *Spiritual Perspectives and Human Facts*. Translated by Peter N. Townsend. Pates Manor: Perennial Books, 1987.

———. *Stations of Wisdom*. Bloomington, Ind.: World Wisdom Books, 1995.

Sulami, Abu 'Abd al-Rahman Muhammad, al-. *Tabaqât al-sufiyya*. Cairo: Maktaba al-Khânjî, 1986.

Tabarānī, Abu 'l Kāsim Sulaymān, al-. *Al-Mū'djam al-kabīr*. 25 vols. Baghdâd: Wuzâra al-awqâf, silsila ihyâ' al-turâth, 1398–1404,

Tabarsi, Hassan ibn Fazl ibn Hassan. *Mishkat ul-Anwar fi Ghurar il-Akhbar*. Translated by Lisa Zaynab Morgan and Ali Peiravi. Qum, Iran: Ansariyan Publications, 2002.

The Thompson Chain-Reference Bible: King James Version. Indianapolis: B. B. Kirkbride Bible Company, 1988.

Tirmidhi, al-Hakim al-. "Sufi Psychological Treatise." Translated by Nicholas Heer. *Muslim World* 51 (1961): 244–46.

Zayn al-'Abidin, 'Ali ibn al-Husayn, Imam. *The Psalms of Islam: Al-Sahīfat al-Kāmilat Al-Sajjādiyya*. Translated by William C. Chittick. Qum, Iran: Ansariyan Publications, 1987.

THE ABRAHAMIC DIALOGUES SERIES

David B. Burrell, series editor

Donald Moore, *Martin Buber: Prophet of Religious Secularism*

James L. Heft, ed., *Beyond Violence: Religious Sources of Social Transformation in Judaism, Christianity, and Islam*

Rusmir Mahmutćehajić, *Learning from Bosnia: Approaching Tradition*

Rusmir Mahmutćehajić, *The Mosque: The Heart of Submission*

Alain Marchadour and David Neuhaus, *The Land, the Bible, and History: Toward the Land That I Will Show You*

James L. Heft, ed., *Passing on the Faith: Transforming Traditions for the Next Generation of Jews, Christians, and Muslims*